An Ocean Between Us

An Ocean Between Us

Evelyn Iritani

William Morrow and Company, Inc. • New York

It is the policy of
William Morrow and Company, Inc.,
and its imprints and affiliates,
recognizing the importance of preserving
what has been written, to print the books we publish
on acid-free paper, and we exert our
best efforts to that end.

Library of Congress Cataloging-in-Publication Data

Iritani, Evelyn.
    An ocean between us / Evelyn Iritani.
        p.   cm.
    ISBN 0-688-10812-1
    1. Washington (State)—Relations—Japan. 2. Japan—Relations—
Washington (State). I. Title.
F891.I73   1994
303.48'2520797—dc20   93-48143
                                                              CIP

Printed in the United States of America

First Edition

1   2   3   4   5   6   7   8   9   10

BOOK DESIGN BY LINEY LI

To Roger, Shaara, and Nicholas

To my parents, Willy and Eiko Iritani

With love and gratitude

Note to
the Reader

F

OR THEIR IN-DEPTH RESEARCH on Port Angeles, Washington, I would like to thank Paul Martin and Peggy Brady, authors of *Port Angeles, Washington: A History* (Port Angeles, Wash.: Peninsula Publishing, 1983), and the archives of the Port Angeles Library.

In the first chapter, I am greatly indebted to three sources for their accounting of the wreck of the *Hojun-maru*: Katherine Plummer's book *The Shogun's Reluctant Ambassadors: Japanese Sea Drifters in the North Pacific* (Portland, Ore.: Oregon Historical Society Press, 1991), Charles Wolcott Brooks's *Japanese*

Wrecks Stranded and Picked Up Adrift in the North Pacific Ocean (Fairfield, Wash.: Ye Galleon Press, 1964) and an article by University of Oregon professor Stephen Kohl ("Strangers in a Strange Land," *Pacific Northwest Quarterly* [January 1982]: 20–28). For her explanation of Makah history and culture, I thank Maria Parker-Pascua, author of *Ozette: A Makah Village in 1941* (*National Geographic* 80, no. 4 [October 1991]: 38–53).

In the third chapter, I benefited greatly from the work of Bert Webber, author of *Retaliation: Japanese Attacks and Allied Countermeasures on the Pacific Coast in World War II* (Corvallis: Oregon State University Press, 1975), and Robert Mikesh, author of *Japan's World War II Balloon Bomb Attacks on North America* (Washington, D.C.: Smithsonian Institution Press, 1973). For the description of the Japanese government's balloon bomb campaign I owe much to the memoir by Reiko Okada entitled *Ohkuno Island: Story of the Student Brigade* (Hiroshima: self-published, 1989).

Some of the periodicals that proved useful in my research were the *Seattle Post-Intelligencer*, the *Peninsula Daily News*, *The Wall Street Journal*, *The Washington Post*, *The New York Times*, *Pulp and Paper Week*, the *Nikkei Weekly*, the *Nihon Keizai Shimbun*, the *Japan Times*, and *Diamond's Japan Business Directory*.

Contents

CONTENTS

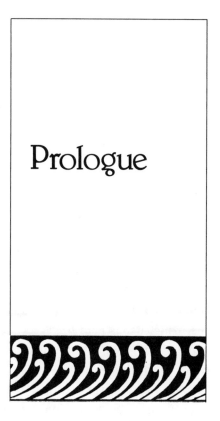

Prologue

FARMERS READ STORM CLOUDS and wind patterns. Dave Hoglund reads supervisors' temperaments, order backlogs, the ebb and flow of the rumor mill at the coffee machine. After thirty years at the paper mill at the base of Ediz Hook, a natural sliver of sand that juts out like a scorpion's tail into the harbor of Port Angeles, Washington, he prided himself on his ability to tell when something big was about to happen. But he didn't see this one coming.

The stocky papermaker had barely walked through the

door of the James River Corp.'s paper mill on that cold fall morning, November 18, 1987, when his relief supervisor walked over with the news.

"The Japs have bought the mill."

"Aw shit," Hoglund thought to himself. "There goes my contract and my job. They'll fire us all and hire back the ones they want at a lower salary. That's how it always happens."

That's how it always happened—in news articles, on television shows, on the magazine racks of the Port Book and News, one of several small bookstores that keep this isolated community of seventeen thousand millworkers, retirees, and big-city escapees in touch with the *New York Times* best-seller list during the long, gray winters. Even for someone whose interest ran to *Hunting and Fishing News* rather than *Fortune* magazine, it was hard to escape the message that a powerful economic machine called Japan was working its way into the fabric of the American economy. Auto plants. Semiconductor manufacturers. Fish processors. From Alaska to New York City, from the skeletons of the U.S. auto industry that littered the Rust Belt to the creaky oil platforms in the sunshine states, there was no escaping it. Japan was coming to America.

Except it wasn't supposed to happen here. Not in Hoglund's piece of paradise, the place he had first laid claim to as an eighteen-year-old kid. Not in this isolated corner of the United States where he—like thousands before him—had come to escape what others called progress.

Within hours, the *Peninsula Daily News*, the town's newspaper, was on the streets with the announcement: Daishowa Paper Mfg. Co., Japan's second-largest paper company, had agreed to buy the James River mill for seventy-five million dollars. The new Japanese owners assured the community it would honor existing labor contracts at the sixty-seven-year-old paper mill and planned no immediate changes in the plant's operation. In addition to preserving 300 high-paying jobs, Daishowa immediately announced plans for a $560-million expansion that would double the city's tax base and add 150 more jobs.

In the weeks to come, Port Angeles business leaders would praise the move as a giant step forward for a city whose traditional timber economy was under attack. But like a children's game of gossip, the community angst doubled and tripled in size as the news was passed along from Smitty's Restaurant to Aggie's Restaurant to the bars up and down Front Street. The regulars marched into Haguewood's Restaurant bearing rumors like they were valuable intelligence, reminding owner Sam Haguewood of a time four decades earlier when an attack on a little-known island in the Pacific stirred up similar emotions.

"The Japanese are coming! The Japanese are coming!"

Down at the mill, the emotional compasses gyrated wildly as the news sank in. There was relief that the aging mill—which had been threatened with closure countless times in the past—had been sold and not shut down. There was curiosity about Ryoei Saito, the reclusive Japanese billionaire who was their new boss. There was anger at James River—the Virginia-based company that had bought the mill from its previous owner just two years earlier. And there was a sickening feeling that the economic malaise that had already claimed the American automobile industry had reached the edges of their piece of the rock, proof positive that something was very, very wrong with America.

"For seventy-five million dollars they bought the mill, the equipment, and our souls," thought Hoglund.

• • •

HOGLUND FELT BETRAYED.

Not by the Japanese, because he never expected anything from them. But by his own leaders and his own country—a nation whose future he and many other union members had come to doubt ever since they'd launched a Buy American campaign and discovered they couldn't find a microwave oven or television that didn't have parts from Taiwan or China or Korea.

Like many of his neighbors, Hoglund sank deep roots in Port Angeles because this small port town represented a piece of America worth going to war for—a place with fresh air, clean streets, and a healthy respect for the working man and the American flag. For most Port Angeles people, the day-to-day ebb and flow isn't determined by fax machines or Wall Street hours or the latest Cable News Network report but by the tides, currents, and seasons. Life in this part of the world is governed by the more and less rainy season, the fishing and hunting season, the boating and hiking season.

The Olympic Peninsula exists as a tribute to a benevolent creator, rich with the ecological majesty that drives poets and hikers wild: snowcapped mountains reaching nearly eight thousand feet into the clouds; moss-covered trees older than the Constitution; acres of craggy cliffs and dense evergreen forests where adventurous souls lose themselves each summer, sometimes by accident, in a natural splendor that inevitably draws them back for more.

Driving into Port Angeles—past the scenic viewpoint that frames the lights of Victoria, British Columbia, across the Strait of Juan de Fuca; past Haguewood's Restaurant, the site of a lengthy battle between its feisty owner and the city council over a neon sign that offends civic sensibilities; past the Black Ball ferry terminal that turns the town into a gigantic waiting room on a summer weekend—there are few signs of a city undergoing historic realignment.

If anything, outsiders might feel as if they'd fallen back to a time before the civil-rights movement and the Vietnam War put a warp on America's *Leave It to Beaver* image. A trip along First Street takes you past the dusty window that was Annie's $10 Shop, past Willi-Lou's Ladies' and Children's Shop, a store that promises to outfit you from cradle to grave, and past Naval Lodge 353: MEMBERS ONLY PLEASE. Port Angeles is a community where Safeway clerks rarely ask for identification to cash checks, the waitresses still say, "Would you like a cup of coffee, honey?" and even the local cranks are afraid to call KAPY radio's morning talk show for fear their neighbors will recognize their voices.

For more than a century, Port Angeles has been the end of the line for the gamblers, big dreamers, and adventurers who just kept moving west until they bumped up against the ocean. Among its early developers was a group of prominent Seattle businesspeople who fled to the deepwater port in 1887 in search of a haven free of the "Chinese problem." Developed on a natural harbor that led its earliest cheerleaders to call it the Cherbourg of the Pacific, an allusion to the French seaport on the English Channel, Port Angeles has always been hostage to its geography and climate. Separated from Seattle by a half-hour ferry ride and seventy miles of curvy two-lane highways that snake past spongy green pastures, saltwater bays, and evergreen-covered mountains, Port Angeles was left on its own to grow, or not to grow, depending on the fate of the forests and sea.

But like many towns in America, Port Angeles hid behind a facade as deceptive as the Frontier Village at Disneyland. Long before Hoglund arrived here, powerful forces were pushing this mill town into what would later be dubbed—by critics and supporters alike—the Pacific Century.

In fact, throughout its history Port Angeles carried on a subtle and often hidden relationship with Japan that echoed America's on-again, off-again dance with its Pacific neighbor. While early British and Spanish explorers coveted the spices and silks of Asia, nineteenth-century traders in Japan looked across the ocean and lusted after the giant Douglas fir and firm-fleshed salmon of the Pacific Northwest. When Japan's Meiji leaders opened up their isolated country in the late 1800s—after more than two hundred years of self-imposed isolation—Japanese companies rushed to the Northwest to trade silk and ceramics for logs and seafood; and poor Japanese farmers and students answered the call for loggers and railroad workers to tame the rugged mountains and desolate plains. Except for the interruption of World War II, the flow of bodies and products across the Pacific climbed steadily.

In big and small ways, Washington State—so far from the other Washington that dictates the United States' formal relationships with Japan—has played a leading role in the knot that binds the two countries. By the late 1980s, Japan was Washington State's largest trading partner, with millions of dollars of goods crossing the ocean every year. A large portion of the logs stacked up on the loading docks in Port Angeles were destined for mills in Japan, the biggest foreign purchaser of Washington logs and seafood. Japan Airlines and All Nippon Airways—Japan's two major airlines—were the top two foreign customers of the Boeing Co., the Seattle-based aerospace giant and the top U.S. exporter. Mitsubishi, one of Japan's leading trading companies, was part owner of a company that invented a popular deep-fried apple chip out of the famous Washington apple.

Washington's governor Booth Gardner—an heir to the timber fortunes of the Weyerhaeuser Co.—led the public welcome for Daishowa to Port Angeles in 1988 and was joined by the *Peninsula Daily News*, the mayor and city council, and local businesspeople. When the Clallam County Economic Development Council held a seminar on doing business with the Japanese, the meeting had to be moved to a bigger room to accommodate the overflow crowd. Shortly after the announcement about the mill's purchase by Daishowa, the city of Port Angeles hired two Japanese college students to teach language classes to any interested city government employees. Several city council members, the city manager, and a police captain were among those who signed up.

But while the local newspaper proclaimed Daishowa's purchase of the mill "welcome news" on its editorial page, the letters-to-the-editor column reflected a darker view of the growing influence of the Japanese in the United States. As in the years leading up to World War II, when America's well-being was threatened by right-wing militarists adorned in swastikas and the Rising Sun, the economic insecurity felt by many Americans in the 1980s and 1990s was exacerbated by the growing power of Japan. The dramatic increase in Japanese investment in the United States prompted a flurry of interest in things Japanese—from sushi to Shinto, from quality circles to management consensus. But in the minds of many Americans, the challenge posed by Japan and other fast-growing Asian countries was neither welcome nor benign. It represented a change in the world that threatened the American way of life. In that sense, it was as scary—perhaps more scary—than the battles fought by American soldiers in the streets of Mogadishu or the deserts of Kuwait.

Throughout the years that would come to be known as the decade of greed, the Reagan and Bush administrations' religious adherence to free markets and a borderless economy was played out against a backdrop of growing paranoia about the loss of America's economic sovereignty to foreigners, particularly the Japanese.

On the Olympic Peninsula—where people registered their allegiance with the sign THIS FAMILY OR BUSINESS SUPPORTED BY TIMBER DOLLARS—the Japanese market was viewed as a two-edged sword. The postwar building boom in Japan created a voracious appetite for the fine-grained old-growth logs that are needed in the traditional post-and-beam construction favored by Japanese homeowners. Timber owners, including the state of Washington, happily sold their logs to the highest bidders. By the 1980s, the domestic mills were having trouble matching the prices paid by Japanese trading companies. U.S. mills also competed against Third World countries from Latin

America to Asia that were opening up their forests to foreign timber companies and establishing sawmills fueled by five-dollar-a-day wages and cheap logs. And many of the small peninsula millowners didn't want, or couldn't afford, to install the equipment needed to cut lumber to Japanese specifications.

Giant wood-products companies such as Weyerhaeuser and ITT Rayonier—like many of America's Fortune 500 companies—shifted their attention to the fast-growing economies of Asia as markets for logs and lumber. But by the late 1980s, the companies that had treated the Olympic Peninsula's natural resources like a bottomless cup were about to have the spigot turned off. The diagnosis was an ecosystem in trouble. The old-growth timber stands that were the breeding ground for a tiny spotted owl were rapidly disappearing, and the wild salmon population was threatened by aggressive logging, dams, and over-fishing. Under pressure from a vocal environmental lobby, the U.S. government began restricting timber sales.

At its peak, five hundred truckloads of logs a day were being cut and hauled off the Olympic Peninsula. But one after another, the mills closed their doors: Penply, Merrill & Ring, Inc., Corey & Sons. They were the ghosts of mills past, throwbacks to a time when the supply of hundred-year-old Douglas fir seemed endless and clear-cutting was viewed as the quickest way of stripping the land for the next crop of trees.

Even the two pulp and paper mills that anchored the Port Angeles waterfront—one owned for decades by the San Francisco–based Crown Zellerbach Corp. and the other by ITT Rayonier—were being squeezed by rising energy and shipping costs, a shrinking wood-chip supply, stiffer pollution-control requirements, and foreign competition. First one, then the other, was rumored to be on the corporate hit list. The loss of either mill would have sent the demoralized community over the brink.

•   •   •

UNTIL DAISHOWA CAME TO PORT ANGELES, the ties that bound the Northwest loggers to the Japanese homeowners or the salmon fishermen to the Tokyo sushi lover were so many steps removed that they were nearly invisible to most people in town. The Pacific Rim was a hobby that could be indulged in by those who were interested and avoided by those who weren't. Aspiring internationalists opened their homes to Japanese college students or an occasional young foreigner sponsored by the local Rotary Club. Mormon missionaries, 4-H Clubs, and retirees joined the flow in the other direction, traveling to Japan for a round of Shinto shrines and cherry-blossom viewing. Sailors from Japan, Korea, or Taiwan occasionally clambered off the giant cargo ships that docked in Port Angeles's deepwater harbor to trade containers of T-shirts and electronic components for logs. In the early 1980s, a campaign by a Japanese businessman to start up an official sister-peninsula relationship between Japan's Noto Peninsula and the Olympic Peninsula died for lack of interest.

For every Port Angeles resident who had met a Japanese person, there were dozens more who hadn't. For every person who had jogged past the Imperial Palace in Tokyo or shared a crowded subway platform with a crowd of giggling Japanese teenagers, there were hundreds more who had never owned a passport. The city's ties to Japan, like America's ties to that archipelago nation, extended back for more than a century.

But in spite of the extensive economic and historic interplay, the Japanese remained more fantasy than fact—an odd mixture of celluloid images, historical remnants, and cultural exotica—until the day Daishowa America arrived in town.

•   •   •

DAVE HOGLUND'S STORY, like countless others that lie buried in the daily routine of otherwise unassuming people, reveals more about the complex relationship between the United States and Japan than oceans of trade figures or diplomatic rhetoric or the price of a Sony Walkman.

The official face of U.S.-Japan relations is recorded in a series of presidential economic agreements and summit meetings. The level of understanding, or more often misunderstanding, is depicted in stories about an American president's offhand comment that the Japanese really mean no when they say yes, or a Japanese politician's proclamation that people of his ethnic background can't digest American beef because their intestines are longer.

While the relationship between the United States and Japan is driven by decisions made in Washington, D.C., and Tokyo, the perceptions of millworkers, auto workers, and stockbrokers also play a role. On the Olympic Peninsula, as in other regions of the United States, the relationship between these two Pacific nations is more than official policy. It boils down to a series of individual encounters, often benign, sometimes wonderful, and occasionally hateful or harsh. In the unmapped terrain of human feelings, the villains and heroes are seldom easy to spot, camouflaged in dense forests of egos, prejudices, and cultural baggage.

Like two huge continental land masses, the cultures of the East and the West have bumped up against each other along the western edge of the United States for more than one hundred years, sometimes gently, other times with an unrelenting pressure that piled hurt upon hurt before it finally spewed forth a volley of fear, anger, and ugliness. The Asiatic Exclusion League. The alien land laws. The World War II internment camps. Digging down into these layers of American history, it is possible to see how the United States and Japan are fated to a relationship of great complexity and passion, a marriage of mutual need and attraction ruled as much by the laws of power, race, and cultural myopia as by the teachings of a civilized society. Injustices on either side get filed away in the national consciousness, only to emerge decades later as proof of bad intentions. Misunderstandings are catalogued under the title of white superiority or Asian deceit, depending on which side of the Pacific Ocean they originated. These forces are as powerful as the Kuroshio, the current responsible for depositing Washington State's first recorded visitors from Japan— three young shipwrecked sailors close to death—onto a rocky beach just seventy miles away from Port Angeles.

More than a century later, it is the global economy that is bringing the Japanese to the shores of the Pacific Northwest, in Boeing 747s built in Seattle from components produced in more than a dozen countries. The power is shifting—and the United States no longer has the political or economic muscle to ship the Japanese back home, chase them out of town with guns, or put them behind barbed-wired fences in the deserts of southern Idaho and northern California.

On the Olympic Peninsula—at the juncture where East

meets West—the cracks in Pax Americana are painfully visible. Paper-mill workers whose jobs have been saved by a company from Japan stand in the grocery-store line next to unemployed lumber-mill workers who blame overpriced Japanese log purchases for their jobs' demise. Sports fishermen who accuse Asian driftnetters of depleting the once-plentiful Northwest salmon runs share moorage with the fishermen who supply Tokyo's most expensive restaurants with sushi. The flow of capital, goods, and people across national borders makes escape impossible, even for isolated communities like Port Angeles. Millworkers here needed a future. The Japanese gave them one. No amount of emotional rhetoric or bashing Honda cars or flag-waving will change that.

While U.S. and Japanese negotiators fight over market access and managed trade, the residents of Port Angeles are discovering what the global economy really means. They're confronting their ghosts and, in some cases, burying their pain. They're learning about competing with workers whose concept of family loyalty extends beyond blood ties to include their employers. They are venturing across the ocean and meeting humans instead of stereotypes. And they're discovering that crossing that sea of cultural differences is never easy or quick. It's messy and unpredictable and riddled with mistakes and misunderstandings—from the incarceration of loyal Americans during World War II to the opening of a private letter.

This book—a collection of personal tales spanning nearly 160 years—begins with three scared Japanese sailors washed up on a beach off the westernmost tip of Washington in 1834 and ends with a reluctant Japanese manager who has been asked to save an American paper mill from the industrial dustheap. It is told by the Americans whose lives were touched by Japan: the Makah whose elders recall the "visitation" from an exotic land; the old-timers who still talk fondly about their Japanese spy; the woman who lost her sister to a bomb floated across the sea by a Japanese military on the losing end of a disastrous war; and four paper-mill workers who owe their jobs, but not necessarily their allegiance, to a man whose family fled the bombs dropped by Americans during World War II.

Future archaeologists might speculate how a collection of Japanese food containers, instead of shards of broken pottery and sharpened pieces of bone, ended up in Becky Hall's Port Angeles classroom, or why framed prints of Mount Fuji outnumber photos of Mount Rainier, the mountain peak that dominates the Northwest psyche, on the walls of Port Angeles offices.

It is these things—some physical, some not—that historians and archaeologists of the twenty-second century will face in their quest to understand the shift in the world economy that has former World War II veterans in Port Angeles producing newsprint for Tokyo readers, real-estate developers in Los Angeles borrowing money from Japan to build office towers in Seattle, and Pearl Harbor veterans commemorating the fiftieth anniversary of the "Day of Infamy" in a Japanese-owned hotel on Waikiki Beach in Honolulu.

The relationship between the Olympic Peninsula and Japan, like that of the United States and its Pacific neighbor, is layer upon layer of individual actions resonating through history. The only certainty is that this history will touch lives in ways that cannot be predicted. It happens, as history always has, one day at a time.

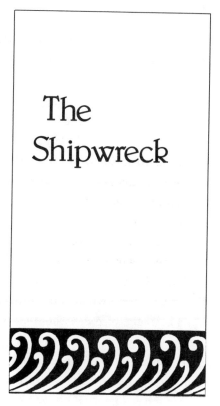

The Shipwreck

S NAGGED ON THE ROCKS off the western tip of the Olympic Peninsula, the odd-looking boat listed to one side, a stunted lady in distress. On deck, three dark-haired men were heaving wooden barrels over the side. The containers disappeared below the surface of the ocean and then bobbed to the top. Soon, there was a miniflotilla—eleven barrels in all—tossed by the waves next to the damaged ship.

Standing on the beach, the Native American seal hunter watched the frenzied activity with great interest. There was something of great importance to the crew of this ship, something floating closer and closer to shore.

The Japanese cargo ship *Hojun-maru* had set sail from the port of Toba, a small fishing village on Japan's Izu Peninsula, in October 1832, ladened with its annual tribute of rice and fine porcelain for the Tokugawa shogun, head of the clan that ruled Japan by the sword from 1600 to 1867. But shortly after leaving the port on the 325-mile trip, a voyage that would normally take just a few days, the lumbering boat was hit by a typhoon. Caught in the powerful Kuroshio, the current that glances off Japan before racing east across the cold north Pacific, the *Hojun-maru* drifted for fourteen months, coming to rest off the west coast of America during the bitterest part of the year, a time when the north winds blow hard and cold.

The piece of rocky shoreline where the Japanese ship finally ended its voyage was home for the Makah, a seafaring group of Native Americans known for its skill in hunting the giant gray whales that followed the North American coast on their annual migration between Alaska and Mexico. Since the Makah controlled most of this isolated peninsula, they were often the first to stumble upon vessels that fell prey to the fierce winds, treacherous currents, and submerged rocks marking the entrance to the Juan de Fuca Strait, the strip of water separating the northern tip of the peninsula from Vancouver Island.

Through the fickle nature of the Kuroshio, the first Japanese known to have set foot in what is now Washington State would not be diplomats or traders or explorers. But while America's early contacts with Europe are painstakingly preserved in history books, movies, and songs, there are few people in the United States who know the story of the *Hojun-*

maru and its legacy on both sides of the Pacific Ocean. Even in Washington State, a place that proudly bills itself as the gateway to the Pacific, few know of the three Japanese sailors cast onto a beach more than a hundred years before Pearl Harbor drove Japan to the forefront of America's consciousness.

In Japan, the stories of the *Hojun-maru* live on. Every year, in the tiny village of Onoura, the descendants of the crew of the ill-fated ship hold a ceremony at Ryōsanji Temple to mark their loss. And in October 1991, the villagers sent Masao Yamamoto—a distant descendant of one of the shipwrecked crew—to pay what became a most awkward thanks to the people who had rescued his ancestors from the sea.

During a time of great tension between the two world powers—a time when polls showed that a majority of Americans viewed Japan as the greatest threat to their economic security—Yamamoto was a reminder that the Japanese haven't always been the world's financiers, alternately applauded as deep-pocketed saviors or vilified as economic imperialists.

In the 1940s, they were a bitter enemy capable of floating weapons of destruction thousands of miles across the ocean to the western shores of America. In the early 1900s, they were cheap labor whose dreams of a better life withered in the railroads and lumber mills and whorehouses of the West Coast. And in 1834, they were three scared sailors at the mercy of a powerful tribe of Northwest whale hunters.

• • •

THE VOYAGE OF THE *HOJUN-MARU* was doomed from the start, a tribute to the rulers of Japan that ran afoul of a capricious wind, bad timing, and political forces beyond anyone's control.

More than two centuries earlier, the Tokugawa clan had wrested control of Japan by killing any likely or unlikely challengers—including the eight-year-old grandson of its fiercest rival—and established its power base in the ancient city of Edo, as Tokyo was then called, while the emperor was kept in imperial seclusion in his beautiful castle in Kyoto.

By 1638, troubled by the influx of European weapons, goods, and Christian ideals, Tokugawa Iemitsu had killed or expelled from Japan all foreigners with the exception of a few Dutch traders who were allowed to do business from a tiny island in Nagasaki Bay. For the next two hundred years, until an American commodore sailed his ships into Edo Bay and used the threat of force to pry the islands open, Japan turned its back on the rest of the world.

The Tokugawa shogunate, as the government was called, had imposed the death penalty on any Japanese who stepped on foreign soil, spoke to, or was seen with foreigners. But the government decided not to rely on the honesty of its seafarers, who were often poor farmers or youthful adventurers trying to make some money. To remove the temptation to sail beyond the nation's watery borders, all ships were restricted in size to 150 tons and redesigned with no keel, one large mast, and a single square sail. The *bezaisen*, as the cargo ships were called, were economical to sail because of their large cargo capacity but were highly unsuited for crossing the dangerous stretch of ocean between Nagoya and Edo, particularly during the autumn typhoon season. Those ships unlucky enough to be caught in gale-force winds often lost their sail and rudder, leaving the crew at the mercy of the ocean currents and Kompira, the Japanese guardian deity of seafarers.

American and European whalers, attracted to the region by the discovery of whales off the northern coast of Japan, were the most likely to come across the derelict Japanese ships. Occasionally, there would be reports that a Japanese ship had wrecked off the coast of Hawaii or Alaska with survivors on board; sometimes they were empty, ghost ships carrying nothing but rotting bodies.

Few people on either side of the Pacific Ocean knew of these early encounters. Those Japanese drifters who returned to Japan via China or Russia were treated like traitors. Although few were actually put to death, most were jailed for at least a brief period. But while Japan officially held the outside world at bay, the government also recognized the need to learn more about what lay beyond its borders. Before being released, the returning drifters were interrogated by government officials and scholars who gleaned valuable information about the way foreigners lived. But some, as the survivors of the *Hojunmaru* would discover, would not even receive this bitter welcome home.

In the 1800s, Japan didn't exist in the minds of most Americans, except as an exotic purveyor of silk and spices far, far away. But in 1875, Charles Wolcott Brooks, a diplomat based in California who served as a representative of Japan, told a group of American scientists that Japanese sailors blown across the Pacific Ocean may have contributed to the similarities between the indigenous cultures of North America and Asia generally attributed to the migration of people across a giant ice bridge between Alaska and Asia.

In his published manuscript *Japanese Wrecks Stranded and Picked Up Adrift in the Pacific Ocean*, Brooks cited sixty known instances of ships that were diverted from Japan to North America between 1617 and 1871. While he and others who have studied this phenomenon could not substantiate the flow of bodies across the Pacific with any degree of accuracy, prehistoric iron fragments uncovered from Native American villages, which predate European discovery of the region, have been traced back to the tool assemblages of ships from Asia.

It is clear that long before the Pacific Century had arrived, decades before Captain George Vancouver and other European explorers began carving out their place in Northwest history, these *hyoryumin*, as the drifters were called, were forging ties between the inhabitants of a tiny island archipelago smaller than the state of California and America's earliest inhabitants. Pioneers by default and ambassadors by necessity, the three young survivors of the *Hojun-maru* would leave an imprint on U.S.-Japan relations: They would be among the first of many to cross the Pacific Ocean against their will and end up changing history.

•   •   •

IT WAS PROBABLY SHELLFISH, not sailors, that the Makah seal hunter was looking for that cold January day in 1834 when he sighted the *Hojun-maru* caught on the rocks. But the Makah, who controlled thousands of acres on the northern tip of the Olympic Peninsula, had learned the value of a shipwreck whose iron castings could be turned into spearheads or where cargo could be bartered with the fur traders for food or weapons.

The Makah waded into the ice-cold current to drag the first water-soaked barrel to shore, calling out to one of his companions to get help from Ozette, the Makah's main fishing village. It wasn't until he got closer to the barrel that he caught a whiff of something foul. By the time he dragged the first barrel to shore, the other barrels were floating up onto the beach. He and several other companions pulled them higher up on the sand, covering their noses with their hands to block out the odor, according to Helma Swan Ward, one of the few Makah elders who recalls hearing the story of her people's first encounter with the Japanese.

The barrels were pried open. The original contents were long gone, devoured by a crew whose sole sustenance in their last months of life was rice and rainwater. Instead, each barrel held the decomposing body of one of the Japanese crew members. According to Buddhist tradition and the dictates of the Japanese government, those who died at sea could not be thrown into the ocean but must be brought back home for a proper burial. Even when their own fate grew increasingly doubtful, the three survivors followed the letter of the law.

Ward, a spry seventy-three-year-old who teaches the Makah language to children, doesn't recall what her ancestors said they did with the bodies, a point that was apparently of less fascination than the gruesome details of the barrel's contents. Others believe the bodies were probably buried somewhere near the beach where they washed up.

Before the *Hojun-maru* broke up on the rocks, the Makah rescued the three survivors: Iwakichi, a twenty-eight-year-old navigator, and two cooks, Kyukichi, fifteen, and Otokichi, fourteen. They also salvaged some of the fine porcelain that was destined for the castle of the Tokugawa shogun. The dishes made their way into the home of a missionary family down the coast.

The wind off the ocean bites deep into the flesh during

the winter months in the Pacific Northwest. The Makah, who originally called themselves the Qwidicca-atx, or "people who live on the cape by the rocks and seagulls," took the sailors back to Ozette, one of the tribe's five villages. Famished and dehydrated from their long voyage, the Japanese sailors were brought into one of the village's cedar longhouses, given furs to keep them warm, and fed dried fish and other foods.

The Makah were hardly the savage monsters conjured up by the propaganda of the Tokugawa shogunate, which, according to Katherine Plummer's book *The Shogun's Reluctant Ambassadors*, force-fed its people frightening stories about the "long-nosed barbarians" in the west, "the giant red-hairs" to the north, and "the black devils" to the south. But in cultural terms, these people dressed in animal skins were an affront to the sailors' religion. Buddhism, which opposes the killing of animals, fostered a caste system in Tokugawa Japan in which the people who worked as butchers or leatherworkers, those who had contact with dead animals, were placed on the lowest rung on the ladder. Even today, descendants of the *burakumin*, or "untouchables," face severe discrimination in Japan and are treated like second-class citizens.

The class lines were drawn very differently on the North American side of the Pacific Ocean. In the Makah hierarchy, there were chiefs, commoners, and slaves. The chiefs—a hereditary title—were the men who were deemed brave and skillful enough to pursue the great gray whale, which migrated north past Ozette in the early spring. The whale hunt was a spiritual, as well as physical, test for the Makah men who prepared for it through fasting and prayer. The whale hunters would paddle their red cedar canoes alongside the giant mammals and spear them, sending one of their men deep into the sea to sew the whale's mouth shut so it wouldn't sink into the ocean as it was towed back to land. From the whale would come meat and oil for food, wiry tendons for binding harpoons, and giant bones that would be carved into war clubs.

Slaves were at the bottom of the heap, doing the same hard labor that falls onto the lower echelon in any society. It was a place in society people didn't elect to join. They were born into it, captured into it, or, as in the case of these three young sailors, drawn into it through a force of nature beyond their control. Day after day, Otokichi and his two crewmates were handcuffed together with leather thongs and put to work gathering seaweed and shellfish off the beaches or herded deep into the woods to gather firewood.

Several months passed by. The three young Japanese sailors from the proud nation of Japan had drifted smack into another proud nation with its own set of rules. If not for the curiosity of a powerful and ambitious British trader, the sailors may have ended their lives in the rain forest of Washington doing the lowliest of jobs, the *burakumin* for a tribe of Northwest people whose days of dominance were numbered.

●　　●　　●

DR. JOHN MCLOUGHLIN, the patriarch of the Hudson's Bay Company at Fort Vancouver, knew the scrap of rice paper was important. It was given to him by one of his captains, who had stopped at a Makah village on a mission for furs and noticed some strange-looking prisoners with olive skin and Asiatic features. They had scratched their names in *kanji*, Chinese characters, on the piece of paper and drawn a picture of their shipwreck.

After receiving the note McLoughlin, a chief officer of the

London-based Hudson's Bay Company and a proponent of using the company's Pacific coast operations as a back door to the silk and spices of Asia, wrote his captains to "do their utmost to recover unfortunate men from the Indians." He dispatched one of his men, Thomas McKay, to try to rescue the sailors by land. But McKay returned empty-handed, unable to reach the isolated spot because the relentless Northwest rains had left the ground too soggy.

On a voyage to Fort Langley, Captain William McNeill located the wrecked *Hojun-maru* on the rocks south of Cape Flattery, where the Strait of Juan de Fuca flows into the Pacific. He stopped at Ozette and struck a deal to buy the freedom of the Japanese sailors. In May 1834, Otokichi, Kyukichi, and Iwakichi arrived at Fort Vancouver, the Hudson's Bay Company's outpost on the mouth of the Columbia River.

The Hudson's Bay Company was a multinational conglomerate run by the best and brightest of Scottish and British society, a commercial empire that eventually extended nearly three million square miles, or one twelfth of the world's surface. Fort Vancouver, named after Captain George Vancouver, the British explorer who mapped the Columbia River, was a frontier cosmopolis populated by fur traders, pioneer families, missionaries, and Native Americans. Outside the fort, there was even a small settlement of Hawaiians who had been brought over to build boats. In the 1820s, the Hudson's Bay Company made its first export shipment, an order of lumber, to the Hawaiian Islands.

The three Japanese sailors—emaciated from their long sea voyage and months in captivity—were admitted to the company hospital and nursed back to health. Then McLoughlin placed them in the care of the Methodist Mission of Oregon, which wasted no time in starting their training in English and Christianity. The Japanese were the subject of great fascination, coming from a country that was little more than a name to most people. One of the most curious was Ranald McDonald, the 10-year-old son of Archibald McDonald (a Scottish immigrant who was another chief official of the Hudson's Bay Company) and Princess Raven, the daughter of the powerful Chief Concomley, ruler of the Chinook, a Native American tribe that originated in the Columbia River basin.

Some argue it was the prejudice Ranald felt as the child of a mixed marriage, others say it was curiosity about his Native American blood. Whatever the reason, the young boy became fascinated with the Japanese sailors, convinced that their ethnicity was in some way linked to his own background. He befriended the Japanese sailors and traded English lessons for schooling in Japanese.

These lessons fueled an intellectual fire that eventually led the rebellious youth to a dangerous voyage of self-discovery. But McDonald's lessons with the three Japanese sailors at Fort Vancouver were cut short because McLoughlin had more in mind than humanitarianism. Otokichi, Kyukichi, and Iwakichi were barter in a game with much higher stakes.

In November 1834, the three Japanese sailors were placed on a ship headed for London. In addition to some clothing and food, McLoughlin also sent along a letter for Hudson's Bay Company officials and a piece of wood from the shipwreck that had the ship's name engraved on it. In his letter, McLoughlin expressed his belief that the crew of the *Hojun-maru* should be used as a wedge to open trade with the recalcitrant Japanese. "I thought the British Government would gladly avail itself of this opportunity to endeavor to open a communication with the Japanese Government and that by these men going to Great Britain they would have an opportunity of being instructed and convey to their countrymen a respectable idea of the grandeur and power of the British nation," he wrote.

Once again, Otokichi and his two companions were at the mercy of currents beyond their control. In London—while the three sailors sat on the ship in the Thames River for ten days—McLoughlin's idea was considered and eventually rejected. The British government was preoccupied with trying to maintain its lucrative opium trade in China, whose government blamed the British and Americans for exploiting the country's drug problem. In addition to not wanting to divert resources from China, the British officials also feared their efforts to return three poor sailors might be considered an affront to the Tokugawa shogunate.

McLoughlin's mission of mercy had turned into a diplomatic shuffle, with everyone trying to figure out a way to get rid of the three young Japanese. Before leaving England, however, the three sailors were allowed a day trip into London, making them the first Japanese to set foot in Britain. The captain of a British ship, the *General Palmer*, agreed to take them as far as Macao, a narrow isthmus near Hong Kong that was a buffer between China and the rest of the world.

In 1835, for the third time in less than a year, the three young sailors entered foreign territory. For months, British government officials and traders sent letters back and forth to Macao, India, and Britain trying to decide what to do with the three Japanese sailors. The questions of cost and diplomacy were complicated by the rumor that America, Britain's upstart competitor for a piece of the lucrative Asian trade, was considering sending its own secret mission to try to open trade with the Japanese. While the British debated, the sailors were turned over to Dr. Karl Gutzlaff, a German-born missionary who had visions of becoming one of the leaders of a Christian rebirth in Japan after the barriers to foreigners were finally dismantled.

Gutzlaff regarded the survivors of the *Hojun-maru* as his ticket into Japan. In exchange for room and board, he recruited their help in translating the New Testament into Japanese. He also learned enough of the Japanese language to hold a sermon once a week in their native tongue. But as each day passed, the young sailors became—in the eyes of the Japanese government—an even greater threat because of their deepening relationships with foreigners and their practice of Christianity.

By the time the British government finally abandoned its effort to repatriate the Japanese sailors, Gutzlaff had located an American trader, Charles William King, who was willing to take the Japanese home on his ship. In 1837, four more Japanese drifters had been brought to Gutzlaff's mission with a terrifying tale of being lost at sea and shipwrecked on an island in the Philippines filled with dark-skinned people. While the voyage of the *Morrison* was billed as a humanitarian gesture, the not-so-hidden agenda for the missionaries and traders was that their humanitarian treatment of the Japanese sailors would endear them to the shogun and open doors for Bibles and business.

On July 4, 1837, the *Morrison* set sail, the first American ship to attempt a visit to Japan since 1807. After removing their guns to demonstrate their friendly intentions, the crew filled the ship's hold with gifts that included American history books, a telescope, and a portrait of George Washington. In letters for the shogun, described in Katherine Plummer's book *The Shogun's Reluctant Ambassadors*, the ship's crew explained their concern for the shipwrecked men, who needed to be "restored to their homes and behold again, their aged parents" and extolled the virtues of developing a relationship with a country like America, where people "worship the God of peace, respect our superiors and live in harmony with each other."

But a portrait of America's first president would not hang in the castle in Edo, and the shipwrecked sailors would never again see their families. Under orders to shoot first and ask questions later, the Japanese chased away the *Morrison* with cannon fire when it tried to come into port in Edo Bay and then later in Kagoshima Bay on the southern tip of Kyushu. On August 29, the *Morrison* returned to Macao with its crew and seven humiliated and angry Japanese sailors. To see Mount Fuji and feel the warm breeze off the Sea of Japan, to come within a few miles of their home and not be able to return, was more disappointment than they could bear. A British official took pity on them and gave them each thirty coins to start their new lives.

Students of U.S.-Japan relations are taught about the voyage of Commodore Matthew Perry, the arrogant American commander who sailed his "black ships" into Edo Bay in 1853, and came away with a treaty that opened up the ports of Hakodate and Shimoda to American ships for supplies and trade. But some scholars argue it was the *Morrison*, the ship carrying the seven shipwrecked Japanese sailors, whose aborted trip to Japan set off an internal debate that forced the shogun to break his county's centuries-long isolation and sign a treaty with Perry, turning Japan into a trading partner of the United States.

Perry's arrival marked the end of the Hermit Kingdom and launched a rush to embrace things Western as the leaders of Meiji Japan tried to make up for more than two hundred years of isolation. Had Otokichi and his crewmates been born just a few decades later, they could have come to America in a seafaring vessel filled with bolts of silk and boxes of fine porcelain instead of a broken-down boat filled with dead bodies.

Otokichi eventually married an Englishwoman and got a job in Shanghai with Dent and Company, a large British trading firm. Iwakichi and Kyukichi went to work for Gutzlaff. At least one of the remaining four Japanese sailors stayed with the ship, and others found jobs in the missionary community.

After Britain won the Opium War with China and began expanding its activity throughout Asia, Otokichi returned to Japan twice as an interpreter for the British. In 1849, when he served as an interpreter for a surveying crew, he told the Japanese officials who boarded the ship that he was Chinese. In 1854, shortly after Perry's visit, Otokichi returned to Japan as an interpreter on board the H.M.S. *Winchester*, a British warship. Admiral James Stirling, commander of the British naval forces in China, was under orders to keep the Russian ships trapped in the Pacific and out of the fighting in the Crimean War. It was Stirling's intention to negotiate a treaty that would prohibit Japan from helping the Russian ships. This time, Otokichi refused to bow to the ground like the other Japanese interpreters. He remained upright and gave the Japanese officials his real name and background. Intrigued by his story, the Japanese officials asked him to stay in Japan, but he refused the invitation.

Otokichi's storytelling abilities were better than his interpreting. Although he had lived abroad for much of his adult life, his English-speaking abilities were not very good, and his Japanese was the variety spoken by commoners rather than the upper-class samurais who were running Japan. As a result, the Japanese thought the British general wanted a commercial treaty, according to an article by University of Oregon professor Stephen Kohl (published in the January 1982 issue of the *Pacific Northwest Quarterly*). Stirling, thanks to Otokichi's accidental assistance, ended up leaving Japan with a commercial treaty that opened up several Japanese ports to British trade. Nearly two decades later, McLoughlin's hopes that the young Japanese sailor would be of use to Britain's commercial interests in Asia were fulfilled.

While Otokichi served as a translator, his first American friend, Ranald MacDonald—who had restored the *a* that his father had removed from the family name—earned his own place in Japanese folklore. In 1848, more than a decade after the Japanese sailors were brought to Fort Vancouver, the restless twenty-four-year-old got a job on an American whaler headed for the north Pacific. There he persuaded the captain to leave him in a rowboat that he had stocked with food and books. He eventually drifted onto Rishiri Island, where he was picked up by the Ainu, the natives who inhabited Japan's northern islands.

MacDonald was turned over to the Japanese government

and taken to a prison in Nagasaki, where he conducted English lessons for some willing Japanese students. One of them, Moriyama Einosuke, would later serve as an interpreter for Perry and American consul general Townsend Harris. MacDonald was eventually turned over to the Dutch, who operated on a small island in Nagasaki Bay, and was then put on an American ship headed for Macao. From there, the young wanderer traveled on to India and Australia, where he made some money in the gold mines before returning home to the Pacific Northwest.

(MacDonald died in 1894 in a small town near Kettle Falls, Washington, where he had devoted the last years of his life writing his memoirs. It wasn't until thirty years later that his book was finally published in the United States, and his story remains an obscure piece of U.S.-Japan history. But in Japan, the adventurous American is widely known as a pioneer ambassador and the country's first native-speaking teacher of English.)

• • •

A PEBBLE IS THROWN in a pond and makes a splash. The number of ripples depends on many factors: the water, the temperature, the wind velocity, the moisture in the air, the shape of the pebble, whether it is smooth or flat, and so on.

A relationship between two countries is like a pond, with millions of pebbles being dropped at any one time and repercussions far beyond their point of initial contact. To understand why the pond and the stone, or two separate individuals, interact in a certain way requires an understanding of the time and place.

Richard McKinnon, a retired professor from the University

of Washington in Seattle, was leafing through some old copies of a journal published by the Asia Society of Japan when he stumbled across an article about the *hyoryumin*, as the drifting sailors were called by the Japanese. Like many tidbits of history that crossed the desk of the Japan specialist, the story faded away, only to resurface years later when one of his former students sent him an article on the survivors of the *Hojun-maru* shipwreck. The second time McKinnon heard the unusual tale, it lodged itself in his mind and wouldn't go away.

McKinnon, who had devoted his career to promoting cultural exchanges between the United States and Japan, was surprised that he hadn't heard more about the survivors of the *Hojun-maru*. He was struck by the way the three Japanese sailors' lives were so radically altered by a series of random events, caught up in physical and political forces beyond their control, fighting to retain their dignity in the most undignified circumstances, and then, in the end, becoming a historical footnote.

In the story of Otokichi, McKinnon, whose family was trapped in Japan when Pearl Habor was bombed, saw a piece of himself. A young man in the wrong place at the wrong time. Politics turning against him. Betrayed by a government that he thought was his own. Because of that, or in spite of it, he vowed to try to rewrite the ending to Otokichi's story. It would not be an obscure footnote in history—not if he had his way.

•   •   •

STANDING ON THE DOCK in Yokohama in his first grown-up suit, a prickly Japanese-made weave that felt as if it was going to melt in the sweltering heat, Dick and his father, D. Brooke McKinnon, waved good-bye to the two young women boarding the ship for the United States.

It was July 1941, and the war talk had reached such a belligerent stage that the McKinnons had decided to send their daughters, Elizabeth and Lincolna, back to the United States. Dick, who was attending the Fourth College in Kanazawa, a small city on the western side of Honshu, was going to stay behind and complete his studies in classical Chinese and Japanese literature.

Dick and his father rode the train—a rolling sauna filled with sweaty bodies—back to their home on the northern island of Hokkaido. When the McKinnons reached Otaru, a small port town on the northern island, they discovered the foreign community up in arms. Two American missionaries in Sapporo, the island's largest city, had been denied permission to leave the island for their annual missionary retreat. Their mail was being opened. They were starting to feel like prisoners on the island.

Paranoia breeds paranoia, especially in a closed-off community. Even the elder McKinnon was worried. The Japanese government—propelled by ambitions of leadership in East Asia and threatened by the West's efforts to stop its expansion—was becoming more aggressive. In July 1939, the United States terminated its thirty-year commercial treaty with Japan and placed an embargo on the sale of high-grade scrap iron and aviation gasoline. The following year, the Japanese government—against the advice of several top navy officers—signed the Tripartite Pact, in which Japan recognized Germany and Italy as the leaders of a "new order" in Europe and those two countries supported Japan's bid to turn Asia into its own satellite, an ill-conceived empire heralded as the Greater East Asia Co-Prosperity Sphere. In a move clearly aimed at the United States, the three countries pledged to assist each other if any one of them were attacked by a country not presently involved in conflict with Germany.

As the tensions across the Pacific increased, the small American community in Japan, mostly teachers, missionaries, or diplomats, began worrying about the consequences of being caught in the middle. D. Brooke McKinnon, an unofficial leader of Hokkaido's small expatriate community, felt responsible for their well-being. It was not, by most descriptions, a threatening group. But in the summer of 1941, it was certainly one that felt threatened.

McKinnon had come to Japan in 1914, recruited out of Harvard University by the Meiji government to teach English in Chofu, a castle town on the southern tip of the main island of Honshu. At the Baptist church, he met Shin Mishima, a young woman from a prominent family of educators. Over her family's protests, who opposed her relationship with a foreigner, Mishima married the young American and they moved to Otaru, a small port city on the northern coast of Hokkaido, where he got a job teaching English at the Otaru Higher Commercial College.

The straitlaced New England teacher, his Japanese wife, and their three children were a local oddity. While McKinnon chose to raise his children in Japan, he made it very clear that America was their home. English was spoken in the home with no exceptions.

When it was time for Dick to return to college in the fall

of 1941, his father placed a call to the president of the Fourth College, now known as Kanazawa University. As a foreigner, Dick needed permission to leave the island to return to school early for a two-week soccer camp. Since the boy was going to be traveling off-island, his father decided to use the opportunity to gain more information. A buildup of naval forces off Hokkaido would be a sign that the Japanese government was readying itself for war.

In order to circumvent the postal censors, the elder McKinnon and his son developed a code, sort of a "childish game," to report his findings. If his son saw anything unusual like a cluster of navy vessels, he was to send a postcard saying, "It was a beautiful day and I had a lovely crossing." It would just be another innocent comment on the weather, a tribute to the polite exchanges so common in Japanese society.

His father, a methodical and cautious man, took no chances. He wanted to alert the U.S. embassy in Tokyo to his concern that the foreigners in Hokkaido were being held captive and that their mail was being read. But he was afraid of the censors. He gave Dick four identical copies of a letter stating his concerns and instructed him to mail them from different places.

On board the ferry that crosses the Tsugaru Strait between Hokkaido and the main island of Honshu, Dick strolled out on the deck and looked out over the harbor. Across the water, in a place generally reserved for barges and cargo vessels, there was a navy destroyer and what appeared to be a cargo ship or transport carrier. For a young man with an active imagination, it was just an exciting game. The first letter was mailed from a box at the train station at Onoura, the next at Aomori, then

Hakodate, and, finally, Kanazawa. When Dick returned to his dormitory room, he wrote a letter to his father: "Dear Daddy, It was a beautiful day and I had a lovely crossing. . . ." Then he put the card in the mailbox and forgot about it. He had more important things to worry about, like that season's soccer scrimmages.

It was impossible to escape the steady drumbeat of war, since the newspapers were filled with the reports of the battles and skirmishes in China. Occasionally, someone would offer an evening of patriotic chest beating and nationalist rhetoric, and Dick would go if attendance was mandatory. But his crowd of friends, mostly fellow soccer players, were more interested in sports and partying than nationalistic rhetoric.

On the morning of December 8, Dick was racing to his first class, an eye-glazing lecture on Chinese history. He wolfed down his breakfast and left his dormitory room in disarray. As he entered the classroom, he could tell something was wrong. Instead of sitting in their seats, all his classmates were standing around in little groups whispering. The conversation stopped, and a friend from the soccer team walked over and whispered the news: Japan had attacked the United States.

Dick's mind jumped wildly from one random thought to the next: What would happen to him? How about his family? Would America bomb Japan? Who would win? His class was called into the auditorium for a speech by the principal, who described the bombing of Pearl Harbor as part of Japan's campaign to defend itself and its Asian neighbors from the white imperialists. Born and raised in Japan but American by citizenship, Dick was suddenly an enemy, in spite of his Japanese blood. Caught between his sense of patriotism as an American and his devotion to the only home he really knew, he didn't know where his loyalties should take him.

After the assembly, Dick was called into the principal's office and introduced to a rotund police officer assigned to guard the city's youngest "enemy alien." The following day, Dick was awoken at four A.M. and taken down to the Kanazawa police station. A few hours later, he was joined by one of the professors from his school, R. H. Blythe, a British expatriate who spoke Japanese with a strong British accent. The two sat in a jail cell for a week and then were moved to a house occupied by an unmarried Canadian Baptist missionary.

Reassured by the Japanese authorities that his parents were safe, Dick tried to settle into a routine. During the day, he and his fellow prisoners read and played chess, a game Dick hated. Blythe, a Zen Buddhist aficionado and music lover, was not allowed to play the piano because it might appear frivolous to passersby. A couple of hours a day, they were allowed to exercise in the garden outside.

One evening, Dick heard a commotion outside. He went to the window and could hear the familiar voices of his soccer mates, who had rerouted their practice runs so they could yell encouraging words like "Hold on there" and "Keep up the spirit."

Early in February 1942, a Japanese officer came to the house and took Dick to a room in the Kanazawa police station that looked like an interrogation chamber out of an American gangster movie. He was told to sit down. A policeman came into the room carrying a sheaf of papers and sat across from him.

After introducing himself, the policeman said he was there

to discuss a serious matter. Over the past weeks, Dick had gone over many different scenarios. But none of his most paranoid fantasies had prepared him for what he heard the policeman say: "I want to discuss the alleged spy ring involving Brooke McKinnon."

Spies were the men in trenchcoats who lived on the screen in movie houses. His father was a respected educator who had devoted his professional career to Japan, a man who had been given a medal of honor by the emperor, an instructor described in the college yearbook as an "American teacher who was very popular with his students for his sense of humor."

The Japanese officer pulled out a letter written to Dick by his father a month or two earlier. In addition to news about family and friends, the letter included a piece of fatherly advice to a rebellious son, an attempt to make sure he didn't get into trouble during a time of tension. The letter began: "Dear Rich, Please keep the margins of your notebooks clean."

It seemed so innocent but when Dick was asked to translate the letter into Japanese, he feared that comment would be misinterpreted. So he skipped that sentence, filling in the gap with something even more innocuous. When he was through, the policeman pointed to that sentence and said, "Are you sure that's right?" Dick had been caught in a lie.

After a round of reprimands, the frightened young man was returned to the missionary's home. A week later, two policemen came by and told him to pack. He was taken to the Kanazawa train station and ordered to buy a ticket to his hometown. The police were waiting in Otaru when Dick disembarked from the train, and he was taken to another small jail cell where he spent a week, distracted only by the scratchings on the walls from previous prisoners. Day after day, Dick was called out of his cell and taken into an interrogation room, where he was questioned about his father: his beliefs, his life history, their correspondence. The interrogations were a verbal minefield, with Dick carefully wending his way through his answers in hopes that nothing he said would blow up on himself or his father. After about a month, the young man was told he was going to be allowed to go home, accompanied by a guard.

En route to Dick's home, the guard stopped at the local police headquarters, where the Japanese government had amassed a pile of evidence against his father: seminar papers, postcards, columns from the *Japan Times*, student compositions, teaching materials. The most ordinary objects were interpreted as tools of espionage—including the photographs the elder McKinnon had often asked his students to bring to discuss in class.

At home, Dick found a guard in his living room and his mother too weak to leave her bed. After the Pearl Harbor attack, when his father was led out of his classroom in handcuffs, his mother's health deteriorated dramatically. Kyo-san, their maid, refused to leave his mother, even after Kyo-san was jailed for a night for her devotion to the family of a traitor. The Japanese authorities wouldn't give Dick's mother any information about her husband: his health, his whereabouts, or what might happen to him.

For the next ten days, Dick spent as much time as possible at his mother's side. He helped her with her medicine, adjusted her bedcovers, and talked to her about family: little vignettes of childhood that have since faded into obscurity.

He volunteered nothing about his experiences in jail, and she didn't ask, nor did they discuss the sacrifice she had made for love, the price of violating Japan's policy of racial purity. Shin Mishima was a private person, who could bring a child to tears with nothing more than a frown and quiet rebuff. Her silence was her strength, and her son had learned to respect it.

On the tenth day, Dick was told to pack up again. His last conversation with his mother was memorable because of what wasn't said. There were so many unanswered questions: Where was he going? What would happen to his father? When would he see her again? His mother simply made him promise that he would leave Japan if he were ever given the opportunity.

From Otaru, Dick was taken to Sendai, where the government had set up an internment camp at a former Catholic church. Foreigners, mostly Europeans and Americans, were brought to the camp from all over Hokkaido. Within weeks, rumors began circulating among the captives that they were going to be released. When a representative of the Swiss government visited the camp to make arrangements for their trip home, Dick was wracked with guilt over leaving. But he was an obedient son, and his mother had given him an order. They both knew she was dying, and his father's future was uncertain.

Dick went back to the United States in June 1942 aboard the *Asama-maru*, the first of two exchange ships that participated in a swap of Japanese diplomats and returnees for American prisoners. The U.S. ambassador to Japan, Joseph Grew, who was on board that ship, told Dick that the government had tried unsuccessfully to have his father included in that first exchange. On August 30, 1942, Grew delivered a radio address in which he described the plight of the U.S. citizens accused by the Japanese of spying: "Among us were many Americans—missionaries, teachers, newspaper correspondents, businessmen—who had spent the preceding six months in solitary confinement in small, bitterly cold prison cells, inadequately clothed and inadequately fed and at times subjected to the most cruel and barbaric tortures."

The elder McKinnon was placed on trial in Japan for espionage in the spring of 1943, but the charge was dismissed for lack of evidence. En route to an internment camp in a racetrack outside of Yokohama, the American professor was allowed to visit his ailing wife for three hours. Under the watchful eyes of a guard, he said good-bye to the woman who had risked the scorn of her family for an American she was losing to a war. That August, while her husband sat in a stall awaiting a ship back to America, she died. When the guards in the internment camp came to deliver the message of his wife's death, he refused to believe them.

On December 2, 1943, nearly two years after his arrest, D. Brooke McKinnon returned on the second exchange ship to the country he had left nearly thirty years before. In a New York restaurant, shortly before Christmas, the McKinnon children were reunited with their father and tried to put the pieces of their lives back together again. But it was an incomplete puzzle, with a gaping hole that no one wanted to touch. The father didn't seem to want to talk about his time in prison, and his children were afraid to ask.

For years, Dick would remember that afternoon and feel guilty. It was painful to look at his father, who was gaunt and pale and had holes where his teeth had been bashed in from the beatings he had received in prison. No matter which way Dick looked at the situation, he felt that he had failed. He had mailed the postcard and letters that became the evidence against his father. He had slipped up during the interrogation about his father's letter. And he had left Japan while his father was in jail and his mother was dying. The McKinnons left the restaurant that day without really discussing what had happened in Japan. The only reference the elder McKinnon made to his treatment, according to his son, was a vague statement that "war does strange things to people."

The McKinnon family, with its language fluency and knowledge of Japan, was a valuable resource to the United States government. After Pearl Harbor, the military quickly discovered that its lack of knowledge about Japan and the Japanese language was a major handicap in fighting in the Pacific. The elder McKinnon went to San Francisco for a job with the Office of War Information, and the three children were hired to teach Japanese to U.S. officers and enlisted men.

Dick joined the staff at the U.S. Military Intelligence Service school at Camp Savage, near Minneapolis, Minnesota. Most of his students were second-generation Japanese Americans, recruited out of the ten internment camps occupied by the Japanese Americans evacuated from the West Coast during World War II.

In an ironic way, Dick had much in common with his students, bright, young men accused of disloyalty, uprooted by war, and forced to reevaluate their definitions of friend and enemy. While he remained bitter about the Japanese government's treatment of his family, Dick made a distinction between his treatment as an "enemy alien"—which he was in spite of his many years in Japan—and the involuntary confinement of 120,000 Japanese Americans, two thirds of whom were American citizens. As a personal protest against the camps, Dick refused to join the campaign to drum up fresh recruits from the internment camps.

From Camp Savage, Dick moved on to Washington, D.C., where he helped Harvard professor Edwin Reischauer decode intercepted Japanese messages. After the two atom bombs were dropped in August 1945, a move that led to Japan's surrender and the end of World War II, Reischauer went on to become one of America's most respected Japan experts, and Dick enrolled at Harvard University to study Far Eastern languages and comparative literature.

For the next three decades, McKinnon devoted his professional career to promoting U.S.-Japan relations: teaching Japanese literature at the University of Washington, developing a program to bring Japanese classical theater to American audiences, and overseeing seminars for Fulbright scholars coming from Japan to the United States. He received the Order of the Rising Sun, a decoration conferred by Emeroror Hirohito in recognition of his "outstanding dedication and achievement towards the enhancement of friendly and amicable relations between our two nations."

In 1988, when officials began gearing up to celebrate Washington State's hundredth birthday the following year, McKinnon saw an opportunity to give the Makah and the crew of the *Hojun-maru* a place in history. That fall, he flew to Japan and traveled by bullet train, express train, and bus down the Izu Peninsula to Onoura, a small fishing village nestled between the mountains and the sea. At Ryōsanji Temple, the family temple of the crew of the *Hōjun-maru*, he found the tombstone with the inscription:

> *Tempo 3 (1832) October 11*
> *Sailed From Toba Bay*
> *Aboard Hojun-maru Juemon's Ship*

McKinnon stayed in the Yamamoto Inn, run by one of the descendants of the family of Otokichi. The professor met with several other descendants of the families of the *Hojun-maru* crew, and also with the mayor and other local officials. Before departing, he suggested they plan a memorial in Neah Bay, a small town on the Makah reservation whose location on a peninsula gave it a geographic symmetry as well as a historic link to the home of the *Hojun-maru* crew. Good-byes were exchanged, and McKinnon returned to Seattle.

Soon after returning from Japan, McKinnon arranged a meeting with some members of the Makah Tribal Council, whose headquarters are in Neah Bay. They listened to his ideas: a memorial service for the shipwrecked crew, cultural exchanges that would bring together young Japanese and Makah, and perhaps the establishment of a reference center on Native Americans in Japan.

At the end of his presentation, the Makah gave the retired professor a polite brush-off: "Yes, over the years we have been told that we had a visitation from our friends from Japan," one elder told him. The meeting was adjourned.

Unbeknownst to McKinnon, Ken Nakano, a Japanese-American engineer, was pursuing his own tribute to the state's first Japanese visitors as part of the centennial celebration. The

Seattle chapter of the Japanese American Citizen's League and Boy Scouts from Washington and Hyogo Prefecture, a region in Japan that is a sister state to Washington, raised forty thousand dollars to install a granite monument engraved with the faces of the three Japanese sailors at Fort Vancouver.

Months went by, and McKinnon grew discouraged. From the Makah, the lack of interest was understandable. He knew that for decades, outsiders had come to the Native Americans with schemes that usually benefited others more than their members. It could be difficult to separate out the well-intentioned from those motivated by personal ambition, greed, or liberal guilt. But since his return from Japan, he had heard nothing from the mayor or others he had met in Onoura. That resounding silence—in a society that exacts harsh punishment from those who fail to repay a personal obligation—was astonishing. "What had happened to those promises?" he wondered?

In 1990, McKinnon awoke one morning unable to move, and the doctors discovered a tumor near his spine. It was bone cancer, but the doctors were confident they removed the malignancy in time. The *Hojun-maru*, like nearly everything else the retired professor was working on, receded in importance.

• • •

THERE WAS NO WARNING to let McKinnon know he was about to be hit by the human version of a kamikaze wind. Just a phone call from a Masao Yamamoto from Onoura, Japan, who said he was probably coming to Seattle and wondered whether the professor could set up a press conference for him and arrange to have the governor of Washington and the mayor of Seattle present. McKinnon, caught off guard by the brusqueness of the telephone conversation, couldn't place the caller. There were no apologies, no questions about the family's well-being, none of the polite chitchat that is a requisite part of any conversation in Japan. It was so un-Japanese that for a moment his sensitivity to social niceties—a demeanor that reflected his strict upbringing—disappeared. Then he found his voice. "I'm sorry, I can't do that. But I will help in any way I can."

By the time he hung up the telephone, McKinnon realized that this high-velocity eccentric was his long-awaited response from the people of Onoura. His visit to Japan two years earlier had initiated a relationship that he now felt obligated to continue, a sort of chain letter of responsibility that could only be broken at the risk of defaming the McKinnon family name.

But hidden within many good intentions are nightmares, and Yamamoto was barely off the airplane that fall day in 1991 before he began to take on the appearance of a big one. Dressed in a black silk kimono more appropriate to a funeral than a business trip, the Japanese trading-company executive was as boisterous in person as he was on the telephone.

McKinnon met Yamamoto at the airport and took him to the Four Seasons Hotel in downtown Seattle, a restored luxury hotel that is a favorite of visiting movie stars and diplomats. Within a few hours, Yamamoto's room resembled a military command post. The expensive wallpaper was barely visible beneath the huge hand-drawn maps of the Pacific Ocean covered with a trail of ink following the *Hojun-maru*'s trail. Above the ornate desk, he had taped a Japanese newspaper article about his trip and a list of Seattle newspapers and television stations.

Yamamoto's leather briefcase was crammed full of papers, including multiple copies of an official proclamation from the governor of his prefecture, the mayor of his city, and the Association of the Manifested Good Deeds of the Hojun-maru to Washington governor Booth Gardner and Seattle Mayor Norm Rice. Tucked in a side pocket were photos of the monument to the crew of the *Hojun-maru* in Japan and several packages of sand, wrapped tightly in cellophane.

In addition to serving as director of the association, Yamamoto also represented the Hermitage of Christ organization, a group of Christians whose members credited the Makah and the Hudson's Bay Company with rescuing the three sailors who helped translate the Bible into Japanese. "It was through your forefathers that the glory of God came to the Japanese people," read their letter. (After World War II, with the encouragement of U.S. occupation authorities, Christianity enjoyed a modest resurgence in Japan, although it is still treated as a "foreign" religion that operates on the periphery of society.)

McKinnon agreed to accompany Yamamoto to a meeting the next day with Japanese consul general Shinsuke Hirai, a veteran diplomat who had developed a personal interest in the *Hojun-maru* story during his posting in the Northwest. Prior to the visit, however, McKinnon called ahead and warned the consul general of his guest's rather unorthodox mannerisms. During the meeting in the consul general's spacious office in a downtown Seattle high-rise, the Japanese diplomat and the professor tried to persuade their guest to pare back his ambitious itinerary. In addition to a press conference with the governor and mayor, he wanted to schedule a meeting with the Makah and a full-scale memorial ceremony on the beach culminating in the burial of a box of Japanese sand.

Later, Hirai, an outgoing man with a fondness for *karaoke*, confided to McKinnon that he believed Yamamoto's blustery behavior, more reminiscent of a professional football coach than a Japanese businessman, was probably due to his rural background. He described him as a "big *koi* in a small pond" who was accustomed to having people jump to his command. But Hirai also felt the mission was "very sincere."

Yamamoto returned from the Japanese consulate determined to go elsewhere for help. He called the front desk at the Four Seasons and asked the concierge to send up the public-relations director. After listening with some skepticism to his grand scheme, she agreed to find him a meeting room but politely turned down his request that she organize a press conference. The rejections were starting to feel like an impenetrable barrier, even to a Japanese hustler with a cause.

By the third day of his visit, Yamamoto began to give ground. He agreed to present the plaque and the containers of sand to the Washington State Historical Museum in Tacoma and pare down his official visit to a handshake with Keith Orton, acting director of Seattle's Office of International Affairs. But he was not about to compromise on the most important part of his mission—visiting the site of the shipwreck to pay homage to the departed souls of the *Hojun-maru*. And it was here that McKinnon and Hirai, who had been drawn into this venture somewhat by default, had the greatest concern.

On the day before he left Japan, Yamamoto had visited the

homes of the most prominent members of the descendants of the families of the *Hojun-maru* crew. He had promised them that he would take a box of sand from the beach near the *Hojun-maru* memorial in Onoura and bury it at Cape Alava, offering a prayer for those sailors who had not received a proper Buddhist burial.

What Yamamoto had not counted on, and in fact had no inkling of, was his good intentions running headlong into the territorial claims of the Makah, who consider those beaches part of their sacred territory. In recent years, the Makah had fought some high-profile disputes over territorial incursions, including an unpopular decision to close a popular hiking trail on Cape Flattery because of concerns that it was being over-used.

Holding a Japanese Buddhist ceremony on a Makah beach without obtaining prior permission seemed like a guarantee of trouble. Hirai and McKinnon, who had spent two years trying to come up with a way to cultivate a relationship between the Makah and the Japanese, were horrified. They delivered a brief lecture on the sovereign rights of Native Americans, hopeful that Yamamoto would be more sensitive to the problems he was courting if he understood the Makah's status in the United States. Trespassing on Makah property, physically or spiritually, would be a violation of the law. Such a confrontation would be an embarrassment to his village, to the Japanese government, and to the entire nation of Japan.

It was, in the indirect manner of the Japanese, an order. Faced with the express dissatisfaction of a representative of the Japanese government and an American *sensei*, or professor, Yamamoto gave in. He agreed not to desecrate the Makah land by burying the box of sand. Instead, he would go to the Olympic Peninsula, like thousands of other visitors who make that trip every year, and just stroll on the beach where his ancestor many times removed had first touched America.

•   •   •

ON THE MORNING of the seaplane flight to the Olympic Peninsula, Yamamoto looked like a traditional Japanese mourner gone awry. He was still wearing his black formal kimono, slightly disheveled after a week on the road, and had a pair of Japanese slippers and white *tabi* (Japanese one-toed socks) on his feet. Accompanied by McKinnon, a newspaper reporter, and a photographer, a small concession to his desire for publicity, Yamamoto made his way to the south end of Lake Union, a small urban lake ringed by houseboats and trendy restaurants, where a chartered seaplane was awaiting its passengers to the peninsula.

Lifting off and climbing above the hillsides covered with luxury condominiums and waterfront homes, the seaplane quickly made its way across the Puget Sound to the Olympic Peninsula. Halfway through the hour-long trip, Yamamoto lost interest in the jagged mountain peaks of the Olympic Mountain range and the lush green forests and turned his attention to the operations of the seaplane. It wasn't long before he had climbed out of his seat and was perched precariously over the pilot's shoulder, pointing to various gauges and meters while holding up a map that obscured half the windshield.

There was a collective sigh of relief when the pilot pointed down below to the tiny collection of houses and dilapidated docks that was Neah Bay, the closest town to the beach where

Yamamoto's ancestors had been blown ashore. From there, it was another forty minutes worth of travel in a chartered van before the incongruous group arrived in the parking lot that marked the start of the three-mile hike through the rain forest to Cape Alava.

Yamamoto leapt out of the van as if he were being chased by demons and ran headlong into a group of senior citizens on an outing in the woods. "My name is Yamamoto, I'm from Japan across the Pacific," he said, grabbing one elderly gentleman's hand and pulling him forward in an awkward embrace. "Japan, U.S., good friends. What's your name?" For a moment, it was as if the entire group of elderly Americans had stopped breathing simultaneously and then whoosh, they all started talking at once, as if someone had pulled a plug.

"Say hello, Bob," chirped one woman quickly, as if the silence would allow this exotic apparition to disappear.

"Yes, say hello, Bob," chimed in her friend.

"Hello, I'm Bob Marks," said the eighty-six-year-old resident of the Park View Villas Retirement Community, an upscale senior housing project in Port Angeles.

Yamamoto posed for a picture with his new friends. Then, using a limited vocabulary of English words, dressed up with dramatic flourish, he fashioned a visual shorthand to explain his mission. He danced back and forth in his borrowed black leather shoes, pointing toward the ocean, and then nodded solemnly before breaking into one of his trademark ear-splitting grins. "Shipwreck. My ancestor. Long ago. Rescued by Indians. I come back. I love Americans. Thank you. Thank you."

Yamamoto looked at his watch and rolled his eyes. His

seaplane would be arriving soon to beat the setting sun, and his mission was far from complete. "By-ye, by-ye," he called out to his rapt audience before strolling off down the wooden boardwalk to the rocky beach, his kimono flowing behind him as he marched, singing old American folk songs in broken English. Occasionally, he would run headlong into a startled hiker whom he would greet with a hearty "Hello, I'm Yamamoto from Japan." And then he would be gone. In a few minutes, he had left his companions behind as he jogged deeper into the rain forest.

What appeared on the surface to be childish enthusiasm was really desperation. Tucked in Yamamoto's pocket was a small sack of sand that he wanted to mix into the sands of Cape Alava before the others caught up with him. He had promised not to bury the box. But his responsibility to the families of the *Hojun-maru* crew demanded that he follow through with his mission even if it meant fudging slightly on his pledge to the Japanese government and McKinnon. By rushing ahead, he hoped to steal some private time to do just that.

By the time Yamamoto broke through the trees and climbed over the driftwood that lines the beach at Cape Alava, the rest of the party had caught up with him. But suddenly, in the context of the beach and the sunshine and the ocean surf, he no longer seemed to care who was with him or what they saw. Facing the ocean, Yamamoto drew himself up tall with his legs apart and began untying the obi that held his kimono tight. Layer by layer he stripped down to his underclothes, and then piece by piece he carefully put himself back together. It would have been disrespectful to honor his ancestors' spirits looking like a disheveled hiker. Occasionally, a breeze would pick up his kimono sleeves and lift them high, like a kite straining to break free.

Yamamoto then scanned the beach for a clean stretch of sand, brushing away the dried seaweed and broken shells from the chosen spot. As the waves crashed against the shore behind him, he knelt down, bowed his head to the ground, and began chanting the names of the crew of the *Hojun-maru*. After reciting a prayer for their souls, he stood up and raised his hands to the sky as if to lift their souls to the heavens.

"Please don't follow me," he asked the rest of the party in Japanese as McKinnon translated. He walked several hundred feet down the beach and turned his back. He pulled the sack of sand out of his pocket, bent down, and quickly mixed it into the sand of Cape Alava. Ashes to ashes, grain to grain. Yamamoto rose, turned toward the ocean, and smiled broadly. He could now return to his village without shame, having released the souls of the fourteen crewmen of the *Hojun-maru*. He walked over to McKinnon and looked him squarely in the eyes, fully aware that his duplicitous act had not gone unnoticed. There was an awkward moment, a pause too long, and then McKinnon grabbed Yamamoto's hand and shook it. "Welcome home," he said to the exhausted man, a marathon runner nearing the end of his race. "I feel I've fulfilled my mission, and if I die now, I will be happy," Yamamoto replied in Japanese.

Behind the two men, the sun broke through the clouds over the isolated piece of the Washington coastline, a favorite destination for hikers trying to escape the more heavily traveled paths in the Cascade Mountain range nearer Seattle. At the top of a small hill that overlooked the beach, Yamamoto turned and lifted his hands high over his head one final time. "Good-bye," he yelled to the empty beach, the sound bouncing across the seaweed-strewn rocks and disappearing on the wind. The sun was well past high noon, and he had one last stop to make in his journey through time, a visit with the tribe that had once enslaved his ancestors.

•   •   •

NEAH BAY IS NOT THE KIND of place that people stumble on accidentally. It is hundreds of miles and dozens of dangerous curves off the beaten track, a tiny town that exists to serve fishermen, loggers, and a few hundred Makah. The town's main attraction—aside from a half-dozen fishermen's motels and a spectacular backdrop of nature's finest—is the Makah Cultural and Research Center, a modern two-story building dedicated to preserving what is left of the earliest-known inhabitants of the region.

The center, a two-million-dollar wooden structure that rises out of the evergreens like a wooden bird poised for flight, was built in 1979, after the Makah became the beneficiaries of a rare gift from nature. In the winter of 1970, a massive storm hit Cape Flattery and uncovered a piece of sixteenth-century humanity locked in a wall of mud. With the help of a crew from Washington State University, the Makah began excavating the cluster of cedar longhouses, part of Ozette, the winter village near the beach where the three Japanese sailors were washed ashore.

Inside the center, the Makah story is told through giant black and white photos from the 1800s and early 1900s, glass cases filled with bone hooks, harpoons, and sealskin clothing, and a reproduction of a cedar longhouse where the recorded voices of Makah elders transport visitors to another era. Its serenity is deceiving. The race to preserve the Makah traditions is a desperate one. An outbreak of typhoid, smallpox, and other diseases, carried to the Northwest by European traders, fur hunters, and soldiers, wiped out two thirds of the tribe in the late 1800s. Few elders are alive who remember their life before the white man, and fewer still speak the Makah language.

It was nearly closing time at the center, and Maria Parker-Pascua, the acting director, was about to close up shop when a dusty van pulled up outside the front door, and Yamamoto climbed out followed by his tired entourage. For just a moment too long, there was silence. Both groups smiled politely at each other, trying to compensate for their inability to communicate, before McKinnon stepped forward. Still weak from cancer surgery, he was feeling worn down by the endless demands of his high-velocity guest.

Yamamoto plunged into his sentence like a drowning man, wrapping a greeting, an apology, and a thanks into one long sentence. He pulled out one last bag of sand from his shoulder bag and gestured to the professor to explain its significance. Parker-Pascua, the great-granddaughter of a Makah whaler, grasped the package as if it were a delicate treasure. It would join the fifty-five thousand other artifacts from the Ozette dig—the harpoons and lances and wooden tools—that were being stored in a large storage shed because the museum was full. No one mentioned the sand left behind on the beach at Cape Alava.

Still standing just inside the door, Yamamoto glanced at his watch. There was a hasty round of thanks and bows, and on the way out the door, he mentioned his hopes to return to Neah Bay sometime soon. Then he was gone.

It was somewhat anticlimactic, this meeting between a descendant of Otokichi and the descendants of the Makah. There was too much confusion for great drama. A man from Japan came to visit. He was apparently a descendant of the family of one of the three sailors who were shipwrecked on a beach and picked up by some Makah. He left a bag of grayish sand. He said he would return.

• • •

YAMAMOTO RUSHED OUT the door of the Makah Cultural and Research Center too quickly to see the engraved plaque dedicated to the members of the tribe who lost their lives fighting the Germans and the Japanese in World War II. Nor did he see how a shift in the world economy was bringing Japan, a country that was little more than an ancient story and some war memories to these Native Americans, back into the lives of the Makah.

But this parallel story isn't visible in the glass cases of the cultural center. It can only be found by driving the dusty street that is the main drag of Neah Bay, past the cutoff to the Makah headquarters (the town's biggest employer), past the town's only restaurant, where unemployed fishermen start their day with a cup of coffee and eggs, past the deserted motel whose clientele disappeared with the shortening of the fishing seasons, to the docks occupied by ships harvesting salmon, cod, and other fish for the Japanese markets.

Neah Bay is the only one of the five Makah villages that survived the arrival of the European explorers, fur traders, and missionaries. In 1855, the chief of the Makah signed a treaty with the U.S. government relinquishing most of their land but guaranteeing the Makah the rights to hunt and fish, rights that have been continually challenged through the courts. The U.S. government's efforts to eradicate a traditional Native American culture considered barbaric and anti-Christian led to the establishment of an "Indian" school in Neah Bay. Makah children were taught that the traditional ways were bad, and the Makah language was forbidden. Eventually, the forced migration of families with children into Neah Bay led to the abandonment of the other Makah villages.

In the 1990s, as in the 1850s, the economy of Neah Bay is a seasonal one. But instead of the self-sufficient life-style of their ancestors, whose daily catch was their nightly meal, the Makah today depend on the markets of Tokyo and New York or checks from the U.S. government to put food on their table.

Aside from the Makah government and the Bureau of Indian Affairs, the Japanese are the ones offering jobs and money to the residents of Neah Bay. Makah Forestry Enterprises, the largest tribal-owned business, markets its logs through Weyerhaeuser Co., which sells most of them to Japan. The town's largest private employer, Olympic Fish Company, of Everett, Washington, sells sea urchins, sea cucumbers, and salmon to Japan.

Olympic Fish Company rents a warehouse next to the Makah government headquarters for the annual harvest of sea-urchin eggs that are exported to Japan. Some three dozen Makah are hired each year at about six dollars an hour. For many of them, it is their first job. Harvesting sea urchins is low-tech, big-headache work. The round spiny sea creatures, which grow on the ocean floor, wear a dark armor of sharp spines designed to fend off hungry predators. Inside that hard shell, beneath a black slimy layer of urchin guts, are the orange, jellylike eggs prized by Japanese gourmets. The work is tedious, boring, and precise. A misplaced scoop or a clumsy toss can turn a forty-dollar-a-pound product into garbage.

Ralph Cox, a twenty-five-year-old Olympic Fish Company employee, is a prisoner of an economic cycle being driven by consumers thousands of miles away: sea urchins in the winter, halibut and salmon in the summer and fall, and government assistance during the lean months. When sea urchin season ends in May, he heads to Alaska to work on a fishing boat. After that, he comes back home and does what his ancestors did between harvests—wood carving.

Cox, a slender young man, is resigned to a future in which the Japanese control the world economy just as they now control, in many ways, his life. He isn't bitter. For him, it isn't much different from decades earlier when the fish and logs that left Neah Bay were sold to companies in New York or San Francisco. Ever since the white man came to this part of the world, the Makah have been answering to someone else. Whether those bright orange sea-urchin eggs are being eaten by rich people speaking English, Japanese, or German, it doesn't really matter.

Just a few blocks away, Mary Hunter is getting ready to go home after another long day of teaching at Neah Bay High School. Over her desk, she has taped photos of some of the graduates of her history classes. They are bright-eyed kids—

many of whom went on to college or jobs—and their successes are a repudiation of the stereotype of reservation Indians with no future.

Hunter, who describes herself as a Native American feminist with an attitude, preaches a worldview in which the history of the Makah nation stands up to the ancient civilizations of Rome or China. She challenges her students to look beyond the boundaries of the reservation at the dismantling of communism in the former Soviet Union and the dramatic rebuilding of Japan and Germany after World War II. As frequently as possible, she exposes them to people from other parts of the world, through exchange programs and field trips.

A year before Yamamoto's arrival in Neah Bay, Hunter's worldview was put to the test when a Chinese freighter collided with and sank a Japanese fish-processing boat in the Strait of Juan de Fuca about twenty-five miles northwest of Cape Flattery. All but one of the *Tenyo-maru*'s eighty-five crew were rescued. Within hours, the oil from the sunken Japanese fish processor began washing up on the pristine beaches of the Olympic Peninsula in huge black globs. For a week, Hunter and her son Carl joined hundreds of other volunteers who swept globs of reddish black oil up off the beaches into enormous garbage bags and captured hundreds of oil-soaked birds for transport to an emergency treatment center in Seattle.

By the time a small submarine sent by the Canadian government had submerged and guided a hose into a porthole so crews could pump the remaining oil out of the *Tenyo-maru*, an estimated seventy thousand gallons of oil had already escaped. The cleanup effort lasted more than a month, and during that time Hunter never saw a representative of either the Japanese government or Taiyo Fisheries, the Japanese fishing giant that owned the processor.

When the Canadian and U.S. officials completed their investigation of the offshore collision, it was the China Ocean Shipping Company, owner of the Chinese vessel, that was held responsible for the accident and was levied a huge fine. Hunter still feels the Japanese—who had such an economic interest in the tribe's logs and sea urchins—should have demonstrated some signs of caring. She knows about the homogeneity of Japanese society and the discrimination faced by the Ainu of the northern islands. She looks at the sea urchins and the salmon and the logs being shipped to Japan. And she fears that the Makah are about to be taken for a ride by yet another group of powerful economic barons.

• • •

A JAPANESE MAN TRAVELS thousands of miles to thank the people who rescued his ancestors and turned them into slaves. The people who enslaved his ancestors are now economically beholden to the descendants of the people they once enslaved. Who is thanking whom? And for what?

Located halfway between Europe and Asia, the Makah have watched the power in the world shift from the East to the West, from the Spanish and British traders with their muskets and liquor to Japanese trading companies. At some point, it doesn't matter from where the money, or the pain, is coming.

But in the smaller picture of personal ties, when an act of human kindness is repaid by a gesture of thanks, a small step is taken with the promise of many more. It is a story that can be added to the collection of oral verse, the day the dark-haired man flew in on a seaplane carrying a gift of sand from a beach in Japan.

A promise is made. The people of the Olympic Peninsula wait. And with each passing day, the Pacific Ocean grinds the sands of Onoura a little deeper into Cape Alava, a beach that is now, as it has always been, the sacred land of the Makah.

Our Spy

MASARU OSASA LOOMED LARGER THAN LIFE for many who knew him, a dark-haired giant with a handlebar mustache, a love of gambling, and a fondness for flowers. He would stroll along the Port Angeles waterfront, a solitary figure smoking his Chesterfields, and stare off across an ocean that pitched and rolled for thousands of miles before lapping up against the shores of his birthplace, in the southern Japanese island of Kyushu.

It was this picture—a lonely man, a harbor filled with

ships, a foreign land—that was etched in the minds of Port Angeles old-timers and would become part of the Osasa legend in the years following his mysterious disappearance in 1939.

Osasa, so the story goes, was a spy. He was a member of the Japanese Imperial Navy sent to the United States to collect information that would help assess the strength of the U.S. Pacific Fleet. When the navy ships pulled into Port Angeles's deepwater harbor during the summer, Osasa would be out there smoking, watching, and calculating.

In 1939, Osasa supposedly returned to Japan to tell his military superiors the bad news. "Don't take on the U.S. military because they are too strong," he pleaded. For that, he was thrown in prison and not allowed to return to the wife and two children he had left behind in Port Angeles. And in the course of modern history, Osasa was proven right.

Or so the story goes.

Port Angeles, a sleepy mill town still waiting to be pushed into the twentieth century, had lost the patriarch of its only Japanese family. But what was a major turning point in the life of Osasa's wife and two children, Peggie and Tom, would register as a momentary dislocation for the rest of the community. The few restaurant customers who cared enough to ask were told Osasa went back to Japan. Most didn't even notice his absence. Over time, his whereabouts became an ugly piece of personal history, a piece of history the family ignored in its quest to fit in. It was a comfortable delusion that could have continued indefinitely if the rest of the world hadn't intruded itself on December 7, 1941, two years after his disappearance.

•   •   •

LONG BEFORE TOKYO BECAME THE CENTER of world finance, the relationship between the United States and Japan veered back and forth between scorn and respect, hatred and warmth, greed and generosity. During times of mutual benefit, the Pacific Ocean became a bridge for money, people, and political favors. The Meiji Restoration, the period that followed the end of Japan's self-imposed isolation, was a giant catch-up game for a country that had been frozen out two centuries of progress. Japan's most promising diplomats and intellectuals were sent abroad to bring back Western philosophies, modern machinery, and even foreign experts to hasten the transition from being a nation of rice farmers to being a manufacturing giant.

American railroad and logging czars and cannery owners looked east for strong men who were eager and willing to work for less than a dollar a day. Most of these early sojourners hoped to make their fortunes and return home. They didn't discover until too late that they had joined the ranks of indentured servitude, a form of economic imprisonment in which there was no early probation or time off for good behavior.

By 1885, when the Japanese government began allowing its young men to come to the United States for work, the population of immigrant Chinese railroad workers and gold miners had already reached more than a quarter million. Japan's earliest exports were poor students seeking Western knowledge, young men fleeing the draft, jobless farmers taxed off their lands, and young women lured into prostitution. Many of the young rebels who made their way to America—some of whom became leaders in organizing Japanese workers and establishing Japanese newspapers—came from samurai families who had been deposed by the Meiji rulers.

The Japanese were initially welcomed as replacements for the Chinese, who had begun agitating for higher wages and better treatment. But it wasn't long before the animosity toward the "yellow races" began to spill over from the Chinese to the Japanese. In 1904, the American Federation of Labor (AFL), a major proponent of the 1892 Chinese Exclusion Act, passed its first anti-Japanese resolution. In his book, *The Issei: The World of the First-Generation Japanese Immigrants, 1885–1924*, Yuji Ichioka chronicled the labor movement's violent opposition to Japanese immigration. He quoted an article in the *American Federationist*, the AFL's official newspaper, outlining the reasons for opposing Japanese laborers: "He will come, stay, and leave us a stranger. Herein lies the greatest danger. I say that our interest can never become his. He cannot be unionized. He cannot be Americanized."

The leaders of Meiji Japan were particularly pained by this embarrassing blot on their international reputation. To prevent its people from being confused with the "heathen Chinese," the Japanese government began a campaign to clean up its human exports. Consular officials were turned into an ex officio vice squad whose job it was to determine whether there were "lower-class undesirables" bringing shame on their homeland. After a visit to Seattle and other Northwest cities in 1891, a horrified Japanese consular officer reported widespread prostitution and gambling in the Japanese communities, supported by aggressive contractors who lured people over from Japan with false promises of wealth and creature comforts. He urged the government to screen its passport requests more carefully.

But the Japanese government's efforts to clean up its overseas image had little impact on the anti-Asian movement, whipped up by the powerful oratories of Democratic politicians such as James Phelan, the mayor of San Francisco, who argued that Chinese and Japanese were "not of the stuff of which American citizens can be made." The *San Francisco Chronicle*, the city's largest newspaper, took up the cry in early 1905 with a series of stories: "Japanese a Menace to American Women," "The Yellow Peril—How Japanese Crowd Out the White Race," and "Brown Men Are an Evil in the Public Schools."

Shortly after the San Francisco earthquake in April 1906, the city's school board finally gained enough votes to pass a resolution ordering Japanese children to attend Chinese schools. That move brought the West Coast nativists into direct conflict with U.S. president Theodore Roosevelt, who was trying to placate Japan's leaders after their surprise victory in the Russo-Japanese War.

The clout Japan was able to wield as a result of its increased international stature—boosted by its alliance with the British in quelling the Boxer Rebellion in China and its signing of the Anglo-Japanese Friendship Treaty in 1907—could be measured in the way its people were treated in the United States. Roosevelt rose up as a defender of the Japanese against the bigots who ruled the West—even as he continued to call the Chinese "undesirable immigrants" because of their willingness to work for low wages and their low standard of living. In his December 1906 State of the Union address, the president termed the hostility toward the Japanese "discreditable" and an unfair attack on their efficiency.

In the end, Roosevelt persuaded the California governor, the state legislature, and the San Francisco leaders to allow the United States and Japan to come to their own agreement.

Congress passed a law that stopped Japanese in Hawaii from migrating onto the mainland. And over the course of two years—1907 to 1908—the two countries reached a political compromise that was designed to cut off most immigration from Japan.

The Gentlemen's Agreement, as it was called, stipulated that the Japanese government would not issue passports valid for the continental United States to laborers, skilled or unskilled. Laborers who had already been to the United States could return, and passports would be issued to families of laborers already in the United States.

The agreement was sold to Americans as an end to the "Japanese problem." But as is often true, avenues for entry into the United States from Japan were still open for those with money, connections or intellect. Passports were falsified or sold. Fake family relationships were created. Most significantly for the Japanese-American population, Japanese men were able to bring in wives and start families. The Chinese, on the other hand, were not allowed to bring in wives. As a result, the Japanese population in the mainland United States increased from 72,157 in 1910 to 111,010 in 1920.

Most of the Japanese immigrants to the Northwest disappeared into logging and railroad camps. By 1907, close to two-thirds of the Japanese men in Washington were employed in logging, sawmills, and railroad crews. One of those who made his way to America was Masaru Osasa, an ambitious man seeking a second chance.

•   •   •

OSASA WAS A PROMISING YOUNG CAPTAIN in the Japanese Imperial Army when he took a weekend furlough with another young officer, according to family legend. The two sat down to rest in the woods, and Osasa's gun accidentally went off, killing his companion. In the retelling, the bullet was a tragic accident, a trajectory of doom with no witnesses. The poor farmer from Kyushu, his military career in ruins, was forced to leave the army in disgrace. In 1911 he decided to go to the United States and make his fortune.

Osasa did not find a city awash with brotherly love toward the "yellow race." Seattle's public leaders—from city hall to the union bosses—had taken up the nativist campaign, and the local newspapers were filled with stories about the dangers of allowing Chinese and Japanese to share the same breathing space as people of European extraction. Just three years earlier, the Asiatic Exclusion League of North America, an anti-Asian pressure organization composed largely of conservative labor groups, held its first and last international convention in Seattle.

Court documents and history books contain the names of Japanese immigrants who fought the discrimination and hatred, the ones who formed their own labor unions or filed lawsuits protesting the restrictive immigration laws and the bans on ownership of land by foreigners, which, by default, included all Japanese immigrants, since they were not allowed citizenship.

But like most of the silent majority, Osasa made his money where he could and moved on when things got bad. He started working in the canneries and gold mines of Alaska before moving south to Washington to work as a foreman on a railroad crew. When Osasa decided he needed a second wife—his family in the United States never determined what happened to the woman he married and left back in Japan—he wrote a letter home to his family asking for help. They located Chi-yono Nishihara, a twenty-year-old woman who had been or-phaned in her teens and had raised her two younger sisters.

When Chiyono walked off the ship in the port of Seattle, she glanced around at the crowd for the handsome man fea-tured in the picture sent by Osasa. She didn't see him any-where on the dock. And then she noticed a much older Japanese man looking at her, a man old enough to be her father. It was him. Fearful that he would not be able to attract a good wife with the truth, Osasa had told her that he was only ten years older than she was when he was really twenty years her senior. It was, in the days of the picture brides, not an uncommon deception. Desperate, lonely men, afraid of rejec-tion, sent their prospective spouses borrowed pictures or let-ters written by someone else. They changed their age, their occupation—anything that might scare off a wife.

The couple traveled all day to reach a railroad camp in the inland plateau of eastern Washington where Osasa was a sec-tion foreman. "You must get up tomorrow morning at four A.M. and make breakfast for a hundred men," he told his new wife, who spoke no English and had only cooked for her family.

Chiyono spent her first night as a bride surrounded by disappointment: miles of rolling hills covered with sagebrush and scrub trees; people who spoke a language she could not understand, and men like her husband who felt their only hope for happiness was a white lie to a pretty girl back home. Welcome to America, land of heartbreak. It was a prison of her own making, and she could see no way of escape.

A man with an eye for opportunity, Osasa soon moved his

wife to Seattle. There he spent the years before the Great Depression working the Skid Road hotel market like a giant Monopoly game. He sent Chiyono to barber school and put her to work cutting hair in one of several downtown hotels he bought and sold. First-generation Japanese immigrants were not allowed to own land under the state constitution. But Osasa, like many other Japanese, apparently found a way around that prohibition. Sometimes people used Caucasians as go-betweens; other times they put the land in their children's names.

Business was good enough that the Osasas took a voyage back to Japan with their two young children in 1921. Chiyono was pregnant with a third child; Peggie was four years old at the time, and her younger sister, Chizue, was just a toddler. During the voyage, Chizue became ill, and she died shortly after their arrival in Fukuoka.

Chiyono was heartbroken. Osasa returned to the United States, but his young wife stayed in Japan long enough to give birth to a baby boy, Frank. Convinced that the long ocean voyage was to blame for the death of her daughter, Chiyono asked her sister to keep the newborn until she could return to Japan for him. At Osasa's insistence, Chiyono also agreed to leave Peggie behind so she could be raised in a place more fitting for a young girl. Several days before she was scheduled to leave, she took Peggie, a round-faced girl in a China-doll haircut, to her sister's home and said good-bye. But the night before the ship was due to leave, Chiyono's sister came by the house with the distraught young girl in tow. Peggie had launched a hunger strike in a desperate attempt to avoid being separated from her mother. It worked.

When Chiyono returned to Seattle with Peggie, she discovered that Osasa had failed to register Frank as a U.S. citizen. Without that document, she couldn't bring her baby son back from Japan. For months, she visited the immigration bureau, pleaded with government officials, and even enlisted the help of a local minister in her fruitless effort to bring her baby home. Osasa, who claimed he had forgotten to register his son's birth, showed little concern for his wife's despair or his son's plight. Later, his children often wondered whether his oversight was deliberate. At that time, many *issei* (first-generation immigrants) sent their children, usually their sons, back to Japan to be educated. These *kibei*, as the children were called, were insurance policies for immigrants denied citizenship in their adopted country.

In 1923, a fourth child, Tom, was born in a downtown Seattle hotel to a woman still grieving the death of one child and the separation from another. Peggie looked after the baby while her parents worked. When the children outgrew the hotel room, their playground became the sidewalks and alleys of downtown Seattle. Peggie would strap on her roller skates and go sailing down the sidewalk, yelling hello to the old men who sat in the doorways nursing their beers. Tom played ball in the alleys, always on the lookout for an excuse to skip out of classes at the Japanese language school.

Chiyono's life was her work and her children. Even though she worked from dawn until midnight cutting hair and cleaning rooms, she was the one the children came to with scraped knees or funny stories. Osasa, on the other hand, was a man to be avoided, a tall stern personality with little patience for disruption of any kind, including the noise of a child's chatter.

They would view him warily from a distance as he handed out room keys or worked out a high-interest loan with a fellow who needed cash more than he needed his gold watch.

In the privacy of their hotel room, the Osasa family spoke Japanese and ate Japanese food. But they were surrounded by *hakujin* (whites). While Seattle boasted a Japanese community that numbered four thousand by the turn of the century, Osasa always made his money off the single white men who worked the docks or came down from the fish canneries in Alaska.

Osasa's promising career as a real-estate speculator ended on October 29, 1929, when the New York stock market crashed and the world economy began its downward spiral. A loan shark depends on an economy strong enough to keep the monthly payments coming in; the Japanese businessman found himself with a lot of debts that were not going to be paid and a pile of worthless stock certificates. Shortly after that, Osasa saw an advertisement in a newspaper for a restaurant in Port Angeles. In the great tradition of westward expansion, he decided the isolated town seventy miles to the west would be a good place to start over.

A few Japanese immigrants had made their way to the Olympic Peninsula, many of them recruited to participate in the ill-fated campaign to build a railroad across the Olympic Peninsula, a dream that couldn't rise above the jagged peaks of the Olympic Mountain range. Others were hired on logging crews or found a piece of land and took up farming, a job that was easily accessible to someone who couldn't speak English but was willing to perform hard labor.

But Osasa and his family were apparently the first Japanese to take up residence in Port Angeles, a choice that remains a mystery to his children six decades later. Whether he was running from something or to something else, they will never know.

Nestled against the Olympic Mountain range, the town has historically been a magnet for the adventurous, the disenfranchised, and the rebellious. In the late 1800s, one of the leaders of the anti-Chinese movement, a prominent Seattle attorney named George Venable Smith, chose Port Angeles for his utopian society freed of the "yellow menace." Smith and some friends—also prominent members of the anti-Chinese campaign—traveled the country advertising their Puget Sound Cooperative Colony, a utopian community modeled after some Smith had seen in travels to Europe. On May 4, 1887, the members drafted articles of incorporation and issued a hundred shares at ten dollars apiece.

Port Angeles's original settlers, who had not been consulted about sharing their space with a utopia, were angered by their new neighbors' high-handed ways. But by the time they had word of the colony's intentions, land had been purchased on the waterfront and eager shareholders were already starting to stake out their new homes. The *Model Commonwealth*, the colony newspaper, informed Port Angeles that it was "blessed" not to have experienced the "misery of having this degrading and debasing element [the Chinese] in their midst."

Although the colony only lasted about a year, a victim of the inevitable collision between idealistic vision and human nature, it provided Port Angeles with an impressive string of firsts: the town's first sawmill, opera house, shipyard, schoolhouse, newspaper, and flush toilet.

The colony left its marks on Port Angeles in other ways. Smith, the ambitious founder, turned his sights to a private law practice before moving on to become a probate judge, and later Clallam County prosecuting attorney and city attorney. Minerva Troy, the daughter of colony surgeon Freeborn S. Lewis, became a community leader and was the first woman in the state to run for a seat in the U.S. House of Representatives in 1922, although she wasn't elected.

In history books, it is the emphasis on education, culture, and self-sufficiency that is praised as the legacy of the Puget Sound Cooperative Colony. But the leadership's vision of white supremacy also didn't simply disappear. In the early 1900s, the Ku Klux Klan attracted several thousand people from all over the Northwest to Port Angeles for rallies.

Osasa moved his family to Port Angeles in the summer of 1930, the year the Great Depression hit the Olympic Peninsula full force, bolstering unemployment rolls as mill after mill announced work cutbacks or closures that were due to a lack of business. But the Port Angeles Noodle Parlor, a skinny diner tacked on to the side of a workingman's hotel, was good food for bad times. For two bits (twenty-five cents), the customer got a bowl of something—chop suey, chow mein, fried rice—tea, and crackers. Sake or beer was extra.

Osasa's noodle parlor, as the restaurant came to be known, became a favorite stop for the loggers who came into town on weekends seeking liquor, women, and a good game of cards. Often they would ask Chiyono to keep their money so they wouldn't lose it all in a night at Harrington's, the corner card room. Invariably, they would wander in drunk after a few bad hands and demand their money back, hulking towers of inebriation looming over the tiny Japanese woman. But over the years, she learned not to give in, and they would usually show up the next day remorseful.

To a young girl raised in the security of a Catholic school, Port Angeles offered too many rough edges. Peggie begged her parents to let her return to Seattle and finish up her schooling at Immaculate Conception. Chiyono, a practical woman, had started sending her daughter to Catholic schools because they provided free transportation. She believed the nuns offered her children a safe haven and agreed that they could return to Seattle in the fall, Peggie to high school and her younger brother to first grade.

Port Angeles was, and still is in many places, a town where children roam free with the knowledge that the dangers of the city are nearly a hundred miles away and the dangers of the country are just part of life. Osasa's noodle parlor was adjacent to a vacant lot that was Tom's escape, a place for playing catch, digging in the mud, or playing tag. Less than a block away was the waterfront, where he could launch his wooden sailboat or cast out a fishing line. It was boy heaven—space, freedom, and loggers who taught him a repertoire of dirty words.

At the end of that first summer, the Osasas packed up their children and sent them back to the nuns in Seattle. Peggie was more than ready to put some distance between herself and the drunkards that weren't above laying an off-color joke or a loose paw on the owner's daughter. But Tom wasn't happy about leaving, and it only took a few days before the women in black habits and the young boy from the woods parted company over a "damn" and a "bastard" and a beating with a hairbrush.

●   ●   ●

FOR A YOUNG BOY, the loggers of Port Angeles were far better
company than Catholic nuns with unbending moral rectitude.
At home, the family always spoke Japanese, since the elder
Osasas could not speak English. But Tom much preferred the
language he heard from the loud, rowdy men who would fill
the booths of the tiny diner with bawdy jokes and tales of a
life in the woods that seemed far more glamorous than clearing
tables and washing dishes.

At Washington Elementary School, Tom was the only one
in his class whose parents hadn't come from European stock,
with the exception of a couple of kids from the Elwha Klallam
tribe—"Injuns," they were called by the others. But if Tom's
eyes were "slanted" a little bit or his parents talked funny, it
didn't seem to make much difference to his friends. They
were a lot more worried about how fast he could run or how
high he could throw a ball.

Making money was something for which Tom showed a
knack even at an early age. In elementary school, he and his
friends would go down to the docks and shine the shoes of
young sailors getting off the ship for a night on the town. When
business slowed down, they'd toss dimes. They'd draw a line
on the sidewalk, and the one who got the coin closest to the
line would get the whole pot. Tom had a deadly accurate
throw.

Before long, Tom was able to save up enough money to
buy a bicycle to roam the streets of his new home, a childish
luxury that was hidden at his friend's house so his father
wouldn't discover it. He and his sister had learned to keep

their pleasures out of their father's way, to keep their contacts with him to a minimum, and to do as they were told as long as they were within his eyesight. The best they could hope for was indifference; the worst, humiliation and anger. When Osasa demanded that his children speak Japanese at the dinner table, they simply quit talking. In a culture like Japan's where people avoid direct confrontation, silence was the most effective weapon of dissent.

Chiyono didn't speak more than a few words of English, but she had figured out the economics of a smile, hard work, and frugality. From dawn until midnight, she worked in the kitchen washing dishes, cooking food, and serving the customers. Her regulars called her "Mama," and she made their noodles just the way they liked them. As his wife assumed more of the restaurant's operation, Osasa began moving to the periphery of the family's lives.

Early in the morning, the tall Japanese man made the rounds to buy groceries for the restaurant and carefully tended the flowers he grew in plastic soy sauce tubs in the alley behind the restaurant. In the afternoons, he would take a stroll on the docks and drop into Harrington's for a card game. When the gambling losses started to eat into the restaurant's meager overhead, Chiyono put her husband on an allowance of five dollars a week.

Sometimes, when the restaurant was empty, Osasa would sit by himself at a booth and play go, a Japanese game of strategy, alternating sides. A couple of times, Peggie came into the restaurant and found her father writing page after page of *hiragana*, the Japanese characters used to supplement *kanji*. One time, she got the nerve to ask him what he was doing.

"These are some of the speeches I'll give if I'm ever asked to give one," he said.

For what? To whom? As the only Japanese man in Port Angeles, Osasa was highly visible and invisible at the same time. Excluded by language and culture, the elder Osasas didn't really form close ties in Port Angeles. Osasa didn't belong to the Rotary or the Lion's Clubs. The family didn't go to church. Their customers were all *hakujin*, except for an occasional out-of-town Japanese visitor or the salesman for the Japanese products. People were friendly enough, waving on the street, making conversation in the restaurant, asking about the kids. But the shared experiences of Osasa and the community were so shallow that they could be easily covered in a few sentences.

By the time Tom was in junior high, he was spending most of his evenings in the kitchen. At that time, the U.S. Pacific Fleet dropped anchor in Port Angeles harbor every summer, an event regarded with some trepidation by the parents of teenage daughters. But the arrival of between five thousand and ten thousand men also attracted the attention of entrepreneurial souls who saw money in servicing the lonesome and lustful.

Within a two-block radius of the Osasa's noodle parlor—which was located in the middle of Port Angeles's downtown business district—there were six whorehouses. Right next door was the Norway House, a run-down brothel that employed six women, at least a couple of whom probably traced their ancestry to the land of fjords and glaciers.

The night shift had its advantages. Osasa's noodle parlor stayed open until two in the morning, and it was usually after midnight that the prostitutes would call in their orders. Tom supplemented his income by delivering food to the whorehouses, where he got to know the madams on a first-name basis. They used to kid the twelve-year-old about taking his payment in trade. That on-the-job training increased Tom's standing when it came time for his friends to lose their virginity. Several times, he was asked to provide some assistance to a pal interested in losing his innocence with an experienced older woman.

It was President Franklin Roosevelt's New Deal that provided Port Angeles with the money to build its way out of the Depression. The Civilian Conservation Corps, the Public Works Administration, and the National Recovery Administration put people to work building highways, paving downtown streets, and remodeling schools. On September 30, 1937, Roosevelt himself came to Port Angeles, the first and last American president to pay a visit to this town while in office, and told the crowd of ten thousand that he would support the creation of Olympic National Park, the 860,000-acre park that is now considered one of this country's most pristine wilderness areas.

But for Tom, life in Port Angeles really began in 1937, when he enrolled at Roosevelt High School and fell in with a gang of wise-cracking teenagers who came to be known as the Dirty Eight. They were the ones who made things happen at the school, the team captains, the class officials, the ones that everybody wanted at their parties, the ones that the teachers would look at and say, "That guy's going to go somewhere." It was an affinity for getting things done and a love of sports that was the glue that held them together.

Sam Haguewood may have been the closest thing the Dirty

Eight had to a leader. The son of a local restaurateur who had come to the peninsula at the turn of the century, he exuded the confidence of someone whose place in the community was assured. He was naturally gregarious and a talented athlete, two qualities that went a long way in a small town. Later, he would leverage his talents and his popularity into a stint as mayor.

John Willson—Bud to his friends—was an easygoing kid with a mind for sports, girls, and fun. School ranked low on his priorities, a problem that caught up with him in high school when his grades plummeted so low his parents decided to send him to Saint Martin's Academy in Olympia, for academic and moral refurbishment.

Willson, whose family owned the hardware store, was considered the "rich kid" of the group because his family bought a new car every two or three years. But class differences didn't count for much in a town where everyone seemed to work hard to make ends meet.

Jack Young, whom Tom described as the "best basketball player of the group," was the son of a logger whose family lived from harvest to harvest. In the summer, he'd work in the woods with his father and pick up new off-color jokes to share with his friends.

Bill Church, the son of a prominent attorney, had his eye on his father's career. But his early aspirations of greatness weren't enough to prevent the younger Church from having fun with his friends. They used his home for poker games—in the absence of parental supervision—until the evening they got sick, and one of them lost his dinner in Bill's parent's bed while another burned a hole in their couch.

Bob Stone was competitive on the field but a loyal friend, the only one of the group who traced his friendship with Tom back to first grade. Jim Vail, a slender guy with a wry smile, was a farm boy. It was Jack Ervin, the son of a logger, who provided the Dirty Eight with their escape, a tiny wood cabin tucked into the woods on the edge of Lake Sutherland, twelve miles west of town. On a lazy summer's day, the boys would drive out to the lake, strip down to their underwear, and dive off the edge of the deck that was built out over the water. When they got older, Tom would supply the refreshments— bottles of sake and liquor stolen from his parents' restaurant.

Tom was the "brainy" one of the bunch, the one who didn't seem to need to study at all to get grades good enough to qualify for the honor society. His knowledge of numbers and his love of gambling were a dangerous combination to those who bet against Tom. Poker. Bowling. Pool. He honed his talent for all of them and then would take on any challengers for cash.

When Tom wasn't hanging around Roosevelt High School, he could usually be found working at the restaurant. Osasa was rarely around, but Chiyono never let her son's friends walk out of the restaurant hungry. In her abbreviated English, she kept track of the boys by their fathers' occupations. Bud was "hardware boy," Bill was "lawyer boy," and Sam was "restaurant boy." "Eat noodles," she'd tell them, and they would comply even if they'd just finished a meal at home. When the noodles were gone and Tom was finished drying the last dishes, the boys would disappear into the back room where all the Osasas lived—a space smaller than Bud's bedroom.

In 1939, the invisible man disappeared. Six years earlier, Osasa had been hospitalized with severe stomach pains. His doctor told him he was too old to operate on. To Osasa, that was a polite way of saying, "You're dying." In Japan, Osasa's fear would have been well founded. Even today, when the United States and other countries have established hospices for dying people to interact with each other and their families, the Japanese still believe it is better for terminally ill patients not to know about their condition for fear it will hasten their deterioration.

Some might say that death is the ultimate motivator, at least for those lucky enough to know ahead of time. In Osasa's case, it was a powerful incentive to return to Kyushu and die in the same place where his ancestors had died for generations. He also wanted to go home and prove to others that he had made it in America. To carry off this charade, he needed some props—in this case everything the Osasa family owned of any value. He took his diamond ring and gold watch, heirlooms he had promised his children, and cleaned out the house and the cash register, leaving only a hundred dollars. But when he asked his wife to cash in the family's insurance policies, she refused.

Tom had watched his mother work from dawn to dusk while his father played cards down the street. He had heard his parents argue about the money his father lost in those card games. And he had been yelled at, and beaten, one time too many. So when Osasa walked out the door of the restaurant with the family's meager fortunes, he was as good as dead in his teenage son's mind. When someone asked about his father, he simply told them he had gone back to Japan. Mostly, he didn't say anything and hoped that no one would notice. And most people didn't.

With only a hundred dollars to their name, the Osasas just

had to work harder. As the only son, Tom felt responsible for taking care of his mother and sister. But with Osasa gone, the young man also felt more at ease pursuing the activities his father considered frivolous. A broken nose turned Tom off football, although he served as team manager. But at five feet eight inches, he was a good enough basketball player to make the varsity team his senior year. With Sam as captain, the team went to the state championship in Seattle and came home to a cheering crowd of admirers.

The Dirty Eight were popular with many of the girls at Roosevelt High, but it was a group of younger women, sophomores and juniors, who really captured their attention. In addition to the sports matches, there was ice skating, skiing, and weekly dances at Clyde's Dance Hall, where Tom and the others perfected their swing and ballroom dance steps. About once a month, a crowd would pile on to the ferry in Port Angeles on a Saturday morning and find their way up to the Trianon Ballroom in north Seattle for an evening of drinking and dancing to the big-band sounds of Tommy Dorsey and the jazz drumming of Gene Krupa. At midnight on Sunday, the tired group would drag themselves onto the ferry and catch a few hours of sleep on the long ride home. At six A.M., they would scramble off the ferry in time for a shower and breakfast before classes. As long as he told Chiyono where he was going, and put in his hours in the restaurant kitchen, she didn't keep a tight rein on her son.

During his last years of high school, Tom fell hard for a petite blonde with big soulful eyes and an upturned hairdo. Barb Hinkle, the daughter of a German immigrant, was a high-energy girl with a good sense of humor. She could dance and play the piano, skills that made her in high demand at parties. His photo album from high school is filled with Barb's pictures. "Wasn't that just a wonderful day we had?" she wrote on one picture of her and Tom. Barb was, in Tom's words, "the girl I kept falling in love with."

One day during their senior year, Barb's father took him aside. Neither Barb nor Tom knew what was coming, although the serious look on the older man's face was enough to tell them that it wasn't going to be just another friendly chat. Somehow, between the mumbling and the awkwardness, the older German immigrant asked the young Japanese-American boy not to date his daughter. There was no explanation, but the meaning was clear: Tom was not of European stock. A friend, maybe; but a boyfriend, never.

Tom was devastated. From the outside looking in, it would seem that a young Japanese-American man might expect to be treated differently in a community of white faces. But in contrast to bigger U.S. cities like Seattle, where the Japanese population had its own neighborhood, its own restaurants, and its own bowling teams, the Japanese who migrated to small towns like Port Angeles were often accepted as individuals. In the days before World War II, one or two Japanese families were more of an eccentricity than a threat.

Port Angeles was not a town that had to deal with racial tension because there was really only one race. There was one black kid, Nate Williams, whose father owned a shoeshine operation. And there were some Native Americans from the nearby reservation who had learned to stay out of other people's way. But people didn't worry a lot about who was white and who was not because it was assumed there would always be more whites and they would always be in control. Port Angeles was a town where the son of a poor Japanese immigrant could belong to the most popular group in high school, could walk into any store without thinking of the consequences, and could date one of the most well-liked girls in the high school without worrying about the future. Or at least he thought he could.

When the young couple got together again, Barb was fighting mad. She was ready to oppose her father, to continue to see Tom romantically. She didn't care about the consequences. But for the first time in his life, Tom didn't feel like fighting. It would not be the last time he would face discrimination, but it might have been one of the most painful. First loves, and first slights, are powerful things—especially when they are mixed together.

The wound was reopened when the Dirty Eight decided to make a celebratory graduation trip to Victoria, across the strait in Canada, for an afternoon at the sports pavilion and dinner. Tom, the classic first-in-line kid, rushed up to the pavilion window to buy his ticket. The woman looked at him and said, "We don't let Japanese in." It was just a woman doing her job, a politely delivered pronouncement of second-class citizenship. But for the second time in a matter of months, this boy from Port Angeles had been told he wasn't the right color.

• • •

IT WAS HIS SISTER PEGGIE WHO INSPIRED TOM to think of a future beyond Port Angeles. She helped find him a job for two summers in Kent, a suburb of Seattle, where she was managing the office for F. H. Hogue, a produce buyer. As the liaison between the company and the farmers, mostly Japanese immigrants in the White River valley south of Seattle, Peggie was a valuable employee and was compensated well. On her monthly salary of $200, the going rate for a college graduate, she was able to afford a nice apartment in the city, a new car, and an enviable social life. One evening when she was working late, Tom stopped by her office and was leafing through some paperwork. He stopped short at a bill for three thousand dollars. "What's this for?" he asked her.

"Do you remember those two guys who were in here for a week?" she answered. "That's what we pay them to handle our books."

When Tom returned to Port Angeles's Roosevelt High School that fall, he changed his major from science to business: typing, shorthand, bookkeeping. He didn't even mind that he and Bob Stone were the only boys in the shorthand class. He had watched his mother and father go from hotel room to hotel room, living on noodles and rice, and had decided he would never work that hard for so little.

The Roosevelt High School yearbook of 1941 holds the thing Tom is most proud of, a list of activities so extensive that it could barely fit in the small space next to his senior picture: president of the Rally Club, assistant fire chief, Booster Club manager, football manager, Boy's Club, Latin Club, "A" Club, and the operetta.

The photos of the class of 1941 are, as in all yearbooks, as much expressions of potential as achievement. Future loggers, government bureaucrats, and criminals each get the same amount of space. It is a group portrait of a serene and orderly world and gives no clue that the class of '41 was about to have much of that potential turned upside down.

•   •   •

THE SUMMER AFTER GRADUATION, the Dirty Eight began going separate ways, although it was always assumed they would eventually drift back to Port Angeles to settle down and raise their families. If Tom had cared, he might have paid more attention to the news about Hitler's march across Europe or the growing tension between the United States and Japan. The dissolution of the trade treaty between the two countries in 1939 was being felt in the Northwest, where U.S.-Japan trade had been growing steadily since the turn of the century.

But Tom and his friends were too busy just surviving to worry much about events happening in countries thousands of miles away. If they bothered to pick up a newspaper, it was the sports page to which they turned. Tom and Bob, the prospective businessmen, enrolled in Wilson Business School in Seattle. To cover their room and board, they got a job at Seattle's Sorrento Hotel. Two days of window washing covered a month's tuition. In Tom's free hours, he joined a Japanese-American bowling team and became known up and down the west coast as a skilled bowler.

On December 7, 1941, Tom was bowling in a tournament in Tacoma when a young paperboy came through the door with a pile of newspapers, each bearing a huge black headline that read PEARL HARBOR BOMBED. The papers sold out in minutes. Tom drove back to Seattle and called his mother. She begged him to come home immediately, but he told her it would be at least a week before he could gather up his belongings and make plans for leaving school.

Peggie was in Yuma, Arizona, where she was overseeing a harvest for F. H. Hogue; her boss asked her to lie low and try to ride out the hysteria. "Maybe they won't do anything to you since you're so far inland," he told the frightened girl. But there was no escaping it, this sense that she had gone from friend to foe overnight, through no fault of her own. When she took the produce to the train station, the same railroad workers who used to wave and say hello, now looked away or mumbled "Jap" when she walked past.

Something had happened to every Japanese American when the Japanese squadron bombed that little-known harbor in the middle of the Pacific Ocean. The following night—while America slept with darkened windows and a sense of great unease—the Federal Bureau of Investigation arrested 736 leaders of the Japanese-American community nationwide, 51 from the Seattle area, many of them farmers who had sold their lettuce and berries to Peggie. For days, their families waited and worried as the men sat behind bars at the immigration building in downtown Seattle and the crops in the fields got closer to harvest. The newspapers were filled with articles discussing the "good Jap, bad Jap" problem. Were the Japanese living in the United States a threat to the security of the nation? If so, what should the government do about them?

•   •   •

BY THE TIME TOM got back to Port Angeles, the city had already begun its transformation from a sleepy town of loggers and paper-mill workers to a military encampment. Thousands of soldiers and sailors streamed onto the Olympic Peninsula, whose strategic location made it the front line in the war to protect the United States from the Japanese invaders. Some were stationed at the Coast Guard station on Ediz Hook, the half-moon strip of land that was also home to the Crown Zellerbach paper mill. The army set up a camp at Port Angeles's Lincoln Park, dug foxholes for a camouflaged camp on the West Fifth Street bluff, and sent out the local National Guardsmen to patrol the beaches. A stream of men and weaponry were shipped out onto the peninsula to set up a string of bunkers and military bases along the Strait of Juan de Fuca that flows into Puget Sound.

Lives in Port Angeles immediately began marching to the military's tune. At 1:30 A.M., nine blasts of the city sirens and mill whistles marked the start of the blackout period. Lights out until seven-thirty the next morning, when three blasts marked the beginning of another day.

All civil and military defense units were put on alert. Extra guards were posted at the Crown Zellerbach and ITT Rayonier pulp and paper mills. Planes from Seattle and Portland were sent off on scouting missions after reports that two or three Japanese aircraft carriers and some submarines were sighted off the west coast.

Sam Haguewood's father had been among those who rushed down to navy headquarters the day after the bombing to try to enlist. He was turned down because of his age, but hundreds more men from the Olympic Peninsula had signed up that day.

Two days after Christmas of that year, four Asian men drove into Port Angeles and made several stops at local stores and scenic vistas before heading on their way. The rumor mill went wild. They were Japanese. They were spies. Three days later, Clallam County sheriff Charles Kemp, a regular at the Osasas' noodle parlor, issued a statement that the four men were Filipinos and had legitimate business in town. But Kemp, who was in charge of monitoring subversive activities, was taking no chances. Under orders from the U.S. attorney general, Kemp began asking all alien Japanese, German, and Italians to turn over items that might be deemed "harmful" if they fell into the wrong hands. It started out with shortwave radios and cameras. Then firearms were added to the list. Then it was expanded to weapons or implements of war or components that might be used as implements of war. Also on the prohibited list were papers or books with invisible writing or photographs, sketches, pictures, or drawings of any military or naval installations.

But while Japanese businesses in Seattle and other parts of the country were being vandalized, burned, and boycotted, the Osasas' noodle parlor was busier than ever. Every quarter spent on a bowl of noodles was registered by the family as a sympathy vote.

Members of the Dirty Eight started to straggle back into town, usually with the idea of spending some time at home before enlisting in the military. The streets of Port Angeles were filled night and day with young men in uniform from all over the country. There were plenty of places to drink and dance the night away, but Tom couldn't take part. There was an eight P.M. curfew for all people of Japanese descent.

Of course, Tom and the gang didn't really have any intention of obeying the curfew. It became a game. Sam or Bud would pick Tom up and drive off to someone's house to party. Along the way, if they saw anyone, they would grab Tom's head, shove it to the floor, and burst out laughing. It was funny, but it was also humiliating. Tom was not the type who liked to run from anything.

There were the "Japs," and there were the Osasas. The *Port Angeles Evening News* ran stories on Kemp's campaign to keep subversion under control in Clallam County. In March 1942, the newspaper reported a series of raids on twelve local homes and the arrests of two Germans and one Italian for possession of contraband, including shortwave-radio equipment. What it didn't report was the kindness the sheriff showed the one Japanese-American family who had made the town its home. Roy Kemp, Charles Kemp's only child, thinks the sheriff was influenced by his wife, Iva, a tiny woman with a big heart and a love of noodles.

One night, Kemp and Iva came into the Osasas' noodle parlor for dinner. Tom walked up to the sheriff's table, a young man with an attitude, and lodged a complaint: "What about this damn curfew?" he asked. "I can't even go to a movie." Before Kemp could answer, his outspoken wife broke in and told Tom to go ahead and see a movie. Her husband, the law and order in town, had been upstaged.

On February 19, 1942—following weeks of debate among top U.S. military leaders about the threat posed by the Japanese living in the United States—President Franklin Roosevelt signed Executive Order 9066, ordering all Japanese from a "restricted" area along the west coast to register for transfer to camps in the nation's interior.

In Seattle and elsewhere, the evacuation notices were nailed to telephone poles and posted in store windows for all to see. Kemp delivered them to the Osasas' restaurant. He told them they were the only ones who needed to know the information.

Down at Haguewood's Restaurant, a story began circulating that Masaru Osasa, the tall Japanese man who had left town in a hurry three years earlier, was a spy. When Sam asked about the rumors, Tom was shocked. His father didn't even have a car or a shortwave radio, he thought to himself. What kind of spy was that?

Tom told his friend the story was false. But Sam walked away from the conversation convinced the rumors were true. Maybe it was Tom's embarrassed response. Perhaps it was his effort to make a joke of it.

To Tom, the allegations that his father was a spy were just one more blow inflicted on his family by a bitter old man. Masaru Osasa had certainly betrayed someone when he walked out that door. But it wasn't the U.S. government. It was the family he had left behind to fight for his honor, even if he hadn't shown his honorable side to them.

There was too much on Tom's mind to worry about his father's reputation. As the date drew near for the Osasas and the other eight Japanese-American families in Clallam County to leave for the internment camps, Kemp dropped by the noodle parlor to tell Chiyono that he had failed in his effort to persuade the federal authorities to give her family an exemption.

The shock that overcame the Osasas was soon replaced by attention to practical matters. The business had to be shut down, their home packed up, sentimental objects entrusted with friends. The Osasas didn't have a lot to show for their years in the kitchen, since most of their objects of value had left with Masaru three years earlier. Tom dropped by Bud's house with a wooden Japanese sword and a small shortwave radio, which he asked his friend to take care of. He didn't expect to be gone too long.

In May 1942, Peggie, who had stayed in Arizona at the urging of her boss, got permission from the U.S. government to return to Port Angeles. Her mother wanted the family to be together when they left for the camps.

Peggie wasn't afraid of traveling back up the west coast until the officer doling out the travel permits started issuing a slew of warnings that sounded as if she was entering a war zone. "Take the inland roads. Don't go out by the ocean." Several hours into the trip up Highway 99, the two-lane predecessor to the major north-south artery Interstate 5, Peggie looked in her rearview mirror and saw a police car and a blue light flashing. She pulled over.

"Are you a Jap?" asked the police officer.

"Yes," Peggie replied.

"What are you doing?" he asked.

The young woman pulled out her pink permission slip. The officer's face registered visible disappointment. "I guess I've gotta let you go," he said reluctantly.

Several days after Peggie's return, the *Port Angeles Evening News* ran a five-paragraph story on the bottom of page six announcing that the "Angeles Noodle Parlor" would be serving fried rice and chop suey for the last time that evening. "Mrs. Osasa and son and daughter, Tommy and Betty [sic], expressed appreciation today to their many local friends and patrons for the associations they have had here in the past 15 years," the article stated.

Tom was put in charge of liquidating the family's meager holdings. The owner of a neighboring restaurant approached Tom and offered him a thousand dollars for everything in the restaurant, including a nickelodeon Tom had purchased with his own money. "I'll throw the damn thing away before I sell it to you for that," he told him.

Piece by piece, they watched their life walk out the door. Dishes went for a quarter apiece. The beloved nickelodeon was sold to the local ice cream parlor. For the first time since she walked off that boat in Seattle, Chiyono's days were empty. There were no noodles to fry, no dishes to wash, and no drunk loggers to pacify with a bowl of hot noodles and a quiet smile. Along with those dishes and bowls and teacups, it seemed as if Tom had sold her reason for getting up each morning. Since coming to Port Angeles a decade earlier, her life had been that restaurant. Now her life was gone, parceled out to total strangers.

Freed of cooking for others, Chiyono started to make meals just for her and for her two children. For the first time in their adult lives, the three of them sat down together for dinner. Slowly, as if a faucet was being turned on, Chiyono began talking about things she had never discussed before. She talked about her life in Japan, about growing up as a young farm girl in the southern island of Kyushu, about losing her parents at an early age and raising her two younger sisters. For her children, it was like being given a key to the family archives.

Even sitting there in the empty restaurant, Tom could not accept he was leaving. No American was going to get shipped away to a camp in the desert with a bunch of other people whose only ties happened to be that somewhere, at sometime, their ancestors had started out from the same group of islands thousands of miles away.

Denial seemed to be the best way to deal with it. Tom never talked about being sent away; his friends didn't ask. They were all still young enough to believe in miracles, or at least the invulnerability of youth. He was a Dirty Eight, for God's sake.

The night before he was scheduled to leave, Tom went over to Barb's house. In spite of her father's protests, they had remained close friends, unable and unwilling to find the strength to undo their particular brand of youthful passion. There had been enough opportunities to see each other beyond the scrutiny of adults, but some line had been drawn in Tom's mind beyond which they had no future.

The last night in Port Angeles was eventful only in its finality. Tom hadn't packed because in the back of his mind, there was still a little voice saying, "You won't have to go. You won't have to go." By the time he reached home at eleven P.M., his belongings were in a suitcase and Chiyono was fuming. The time for denial was over.

Under orders from the government, they had packed "bedding and linens, toilet articles, clothing, eating utensils and essential personal effects." On June 3, 1942, the Osasas piled their belongings into Peggie's car and Barb drove them to Port Townsend, where they met up with the other Japanese-American families from the Olympic Peninsula. Some of them, like the Kimuras from Clallam Bay, were old friends who had frequently stopped into the restaurant on their trips to town. Others were strangers. Of the twelve evacuees from Clallam

County, everyone but Chiyono and the Kimuras—who, as first-generation immigrants, were denied citizenship—were U.S. citizens. Of the 120,000 Japanese Americans sent to internment camps during World War II, two thirds were U.S. citizens.

Tom and Barb parted at the bus station, with sad good-byes and promises to write. A bus took the evacuees to the train station in Centralia, Washington, south of Seattle, where they climbed on board a train for the journey to California. Inside the train, young men in uniform joked with their passengers as they came in the door. Packs of cards came out, and the betting started. The stuffy air began smelling like rice and vegetables and green tea.

Black blinds were pulled down over the windows, and the train began to roll. At forty-seven years of age, Chiyono Osasa's sole possessions of value were a suitcase of clothes and her two children. But for the first time since her parents died, Chiyono was going to be taken care of by someone else. Not by the man of her dreams, the one she had hoped would be waiting at that dock in Seattle nearly three decades earlier, but by the country she had adopted as her own, even though it had not reciprocated in kind.

•　•　•

Back in Port Angeles, the Osasa legacy was reduced to a handful of possessions and a bunch of memories. The noodle parlor was empty, the dishes already appearing on other people's dinner tables. For the Dirty Eight, there were no teary farewells or even stoic handshakes. No one even remembers Tom saying good-bye.

People were edgy. On June 7, 1942, Port Angeles went into high alert after a Japanese submarine torpedoed the S.S. *Coast Trader*, a freighter, just forty-three miles west of Cape Flattery. U.S. and Canadian Coast Guard were able to rescue thirty-four crew members of the ship, which was carrying newsprint from Port Angeles to California. One life was lost.

Later that month, fears of an attack by the Japanese were raised again when a Japanese submarine shelled Fort Stevens, a U.S. military base in Astoria, Oregon. No one was killed in that incident, but West Coast cities like Port Angeles were put under even tighter security.

The drumbeat of patriotism was being heard across America, and young men were trading in their cotton shirts for military uniforms by the thousands. There were few conscientious or unconscientious objectors in this group, few philosophical arguments over beer about the wisdom of defending the red, white, and blue. Jack Ervin, the lanky giant who belonged to the Dirty Eight, was devastated when he was turned down because he was an inch too tall. All of the others found themselves in some branch of the service during the first year of the war.

For a generation of young people from rural America, World War II was basic training in life. One of the first times Sam and some friends left their Southern boot camp, they climbed on board a public bus in their uniforms and filled a row of empty seats near the back. When some black people climbed on the bus, they shot some dirty looks at the fresh-faced boys in uniform. Sam was shocked to discover he was sitting in the seats reserved for "colored folks."

The rah-rah philosophy of the U.S. Army became a new

form of sports fever for these young athletes—shooting a gun instead of baskets, running obstacle courses instead of a fifty-yard dash. It wasn't too long before Sam found out that hating the Japanese was as much a part of fighting the war as good marksmanship. But no matter what others said, he could not put Tom in the same category as the enemy. "How could I hate Tom?" he recalled asking himself. "So I felt both ways. I liked Tom. But I didn't like the Japanese because of the type of leadership they had."

News of the internment camps slowed to a trickle after the Japanese Americans were taken away. Tom had disappeared into a no-man's-land of forced separation, as psychologically removed as any foreign country might be. An occasional letter would be received and shared whenever one of the guys would come home on leave.

No one could imagine Tom's life because they had no point of reference for such a place. Tule Lake, California, one of ten internment camps established in California, Idaho, Wyoming, Utah, Arizona, Colorado, and Arkansas, was bleakness itself. Located a few miles south of the Oregon border, in a valley lodged between Abalone Mountain and Castle Rock, the camp site was a lake bottom drained by the Federal Bureau of Reclamation. The nearest town of any size was Klamath Falls, Oregon, thirty-five miles to the north. As far as the eye could see, the scenery was barren and dusty. The camp itself was a row of army barracks surrounded by barbed-wire fences and sentry towers with armed guards. And in June, when the internees arrived, a dry heat broke the hundred-degree mark with some regularity.

Tom, who had grown up with Caucasians, felt as if he had

been exiled to another country. The Osasas were among the first group to arrive at Tule Lake, which was also a destination for many of the Japanese families from the White River valley south of Seattle. Most of the others from Washington were sent to Minidoka, Idaho.

One of the advantages of being early was getting priority for the camp's best jobs. Peggie was hired as a secretary to the camp administrator. At nineteen, Tom found himself running the camp's housing and employment division for sixteen dollars a month. It was one of the highest-paid jobs in camp, but most of his wages went to buy commissary food to supplement the institutional food they were fed at the communal mess halls.

Block 18-16-B was the Osasas' home. Their room, about twenty feet wide, had a wooden floor and walls that only reached part way to the ceiling, leaving a gap that allowed other people's smells and sounds to seep into the only place that could be called private. Tom got some plasterboard and partitioned off the bedrooms. In the front, there was a potbellied stove for cooking and heating. Closets, tables, and chairs were built out of scrap lumber.

In its own way, Tule Lake became a way of life. Every morning after breakfast, the kids went to school, and the older people went back to their homes or to a job in the administrative offices or the camp farm. There were high school sports teams, cheerleaders, and student body organizations. Ministers came in and opened up churches for the "incarcerated persons," as they were called. Peggie's office was in charge of setting up classes and social occasions. She and some of her girlfriends took a marriage course in the evening. She and her fiancé, Bill Doi, worked on the *Tulean Dispatch*, the weekly newspaper that became the community's voice to the outside world.

With her life on hold, Chiyono began to relax. She made some friends with other *issei* women, enrolled in an English class, and began talking to her children, particularly her daughter, about the disappointments she had never shared with anyone before.

While others in the camp grew angry and bitter, Chiyono became more animated. She began attending Catholic church services, curious about the religion that had captured her daughter's soul, and eventually asked to become baptized. In the most ironic way, the middle-aged Japanese woman was happier living behind barbed wire in the desert of California than she ever remembered. But the same wasn't true of her son, who was increasingly disturbed by the unjust imprisonment.

In the fall of 1942, there were already voices within the U.S. government arguing that the internment end, reasoning that it wasn't necessary for national security. It wasn't long before the U.S. government, and the West Coast farm community, discovered how important those Japanese workers had been to the economy. In eastern Washington and Oregon, Idaho and northern California, farmers desperate for field help asked the government to allow some of the internees out to help with the harvest.

Tom signed up with the first group of contract workers sent out to harvest sugar beets in eastern Oregon and Idaho. For three months, they traveled around working for Caucasian farmers for less than what his father made when he came to

America three decades earlier. When they got to their first job, in Weiser, Idaho, signs went up in the windows of all the stores their first night in town: NO JAPS ALLOWED. The crew of young Japanese-American men threatened to boycott the harvest unless the signs came down. The farmers panicked and gave in. After that, there were fewer problems with the townspeople.

By the time Tom returned to camp that fall, the U.S. military had decided to start recruiting Japanese language specialists for intelligence work out of the internment camps. Dick Nishijima and several other friends from camp, guys he had worked with in the sugar-beet fields, wanted him to join up. Tom wasn't eager to go into a war that was claiming hundreds of lives in places he hadn't ever heard of. But he still got occasional letters from Port Angeles, mostly from Barb. She talked about life after Pearl Harbor, rationing, and the guys joining up right and left. Tom knew his friends were going away to fight for their country. He didn't think he could return to Port Angeles with his pride intact unless he had proven his loyalty.

But for Tom, and a lot of other nisei (second-generation Japanese), enthusiasm wasn't enough. To get into the military intelligence service, these young men had to speak and read Japanese. Otherwise, the military might as well be recruiting from Seattle or St. Louis instead of from internment camps in the middle of the California desert.

The U.S. government went into the camps with the assumption that a lot of these healthy *nisei* men, especially the younger ones who had been beating down the doors of their recruiting office since the war had broken out, would speak

Japanese. And some of them did. But more often, they understood quite a bit, spoke very little, and read hardly at all.

(In a traditional Japanese home, where the parents spoke and the children listened, it was possible to fake a knowledge of Japanese. The children learned enough to do what they were told. Otherwise, they kept quiet at home. Words spoken in anger or spite were spoken in English so the parents couldn't understand.)

In Tom's first meeting with the recruiter, he was shown the Japanese written character for people. Tom admitted to the recruiter that the black squiggles looked familiar, but he couldn't remember what they meant. It was a lapse in knowledge equivalent to not knowing the letter *A*. The recruiter was ready to send him packing, but Tom pleaded for a second chance.

Tom was sent back to his barracks with a Japanese book and told to learn five pages by the next day. He studied through the night with the help of a friend's sister. When he returned to the recruiter's office, he was able to translate the whole passage. But he had really memorized the English translation. If anyone had stopped him and asked about a specific character, he would have been lost.

From Tule Lake, Tom and his friends were sent to Camp Savage, the foreign-language school where Dick McKinnon taught after returning from Japan. (Tom doesn't recall ever crossing paths with McKinnon.) Tom was such a poor student that he ended up in the "playboy" class with the Caucasian officers whose Japanese reading and writing talents far outstretched their speaking abilities.

In September 1943, following graduation from Camp Savage and basic training in Georgia, Tom boarded a ship headed for the war in the Pacific. There were six thousand Japanese-American members of the military intelligence service who served in the Pacific as translators, interpreters, and spies. Tom spent ten months with the marine corps in the Pacific Islands, was transferred to the 1st Cavalry Division, and went to the Philippines. From there, he joined the 11th Airborne Division.

In 1943, a series of protests led the war relocation authorities to turn the Tule Lake facility into a detention camp for those labeled disloyal by the U.S. government. In February, the camp authorities decided to distribute a questionnaire to the internees to determine their level of patriotism. The measure of loyalty boiled down to two key questions regarding the person's willingness to serve in the armed forces and the person's willingness to defend the United States and "forswear any form of allegiance or obedience to the Japanese emperor or any other foreign government, power or organization."

The majority of the seventy-five thousand internees who filled out the questionnaires passed the loyalty oath. But for a variety of reasons, nearly nine thousand answered no to at least one of the two key questions. In his book *Asian America: Chinese and Japanese in the United States Since 1850* Roger Daniels described the questionnaire as inappropriate, misleading, and poorly administered. He said those who ended up labeled "disloyal" and shipped to Tule Lake included many who were confused, ambivalent, or simply seeking a way to register their disillusionment. In time, however, the prison camp atmosphere at Tule Lake turned skepticism and mistrust into hatred, prompting more than one third of the camp's population to make formal applications to return to Japan.

On the advice of her children, Chiyono answered yes to both questions and was shipped off to Minidoka, an internment camp in southern Idaho. About a year later, she was allowed to leave for a job in Rockford, Illinois, which was set up for her by some friends who had left camp earlier. Peggie, who had left Tule Lake earlier to get married, ended up in Minneapolis, where her husband and her brother were attending Japanese language school.

By the time the internment camps were officially closed down in 1945 and 1946, many of the internees already had left the camps for jobs or schools in the Midwest and East Coast. But thousands of others finally had to be forcibly evicted, refusing to leave because they feared for their safety or had no place to go.

There were a number of occasions during his time in the Pacific when Tom wished he had obeyed his father and learned Japanese. Back then, it had been a matter of childish stubbornness. Now, it was a matter of survival.

Tom's chief job was interrogating prisoners, since his language skills couldn't really be trusted for translating diaries or captured documents. His friend, Dick Nishijima, ended up accompanying Ernie Pyle, the World War II journalist who brought the war home to America. Once, Tom was working alone because his partner, a Hawaiian named Ryochi Okada, had to do something back at headquarters. The camp intercepted some messages and Tom interpreted them to mean the Japanese were going to attack at five P.M. When Okada returned that afternoon, he found machine gun nests set up around the perimeter of the camp.

"What's going on?" he asked. Tom showed him the note.

"Hell, this says we're going to attack them," Okada said.

Luckily, no one but Tom and his partner ever found out about the screwup, and no one died because of it. And he had the satisfaction of knowing that the Japanese soldier who sent the note was just as wrong as he was.

Tom didn't have any trouble thinking of the Japanese as the enemy. He didn't look at his prisoner during an interrogation and think, "You could be my cousin or my brother." He couldn't afford to.

The exploits of Port Angeles's only Japanese-American soldier made their way back home in letters to the Dirty Eight and Barb, who was able to get some of them printed in the local newspaper. One column included the following: "Sergeant Tommy Osasa, formerly Port Angeles high school student, writes from the Philippines that entering Manila with the First Calvary Division [the first American forces to enter the battered capital] made a 'believer' out of him. He had to sweat out a number of nights of artillery, mortar and rocket fire, which was anything but pleasant, he says."

By the end of the war, twenty-three thousand Japanese Americans had served in the military. In addition to the military intelligence service (MIS), thousands of mainland and Hawaiian *nisei* joined the 100/442nd Battalion, which emerged from battles in Italy and France as the most decorated unit in American history. General Charles Willoughby, General Douglas MacArthur's intelligence chief, credited the MIS with shortening the war by two years.

On August 14, 1945, the Japanese surrendered to the United States; Tom was assigned to the 11th Airborne that accompanied General MacArthur to Japan. On August 30, the young Japanese American from Port Angeles climbed into a jeep that accompanied the famous U.S. military commander on the twenty-mile ride from Atsugi Air Base to the New Grand Hotel in Yokohama.

Tom's first sight of Japan, the land of his forefathers, was a scene out of a science-fiction movie: mile after mile of flattened buildings and no women or children anywhere. They had been sent away for fear the American soldiers would rape and kill them. The road from the air base to Yokohama was lined with hundreds of Japanese soldiers, most of them with their backs to the procession to show their subservience.

Once again, the Japanese Americans found themselves on the wrong side of the war. While the Caucasian soldiers, the Western conquerors, were held in awe by the Japanese people, the U.S. soldiers with Japanese faces were considered traitors. Many days, Tom felt as if no one trusted him.

As winter came, the desperation increased in Yokohama and other big Japanese cities. Driving officers to and from work, Tom would see people scrounging through garbage for food and scraps of wood or metal to build makeshift homes. People in need of warmth would try to buy the clothes off the backs of the American soldiers.

Inspired by some of his friends, who were able to locate their relatives in Japan, Tom decided it was time to end the war with his father. He wrote home to his mother and asked her for his father's and brother's address. Weeks passed by with no reply. Chiyono was afraid her son would get in trouble for contacting the enemy.

But Tom asked again, and his mother finally gave in. He wrote his brother and father at their last known addresses. Then he waited, turning down two chances to return to the

United States in hopes that he would get a response. In November 1945, he gave up and returned home to Minnesota, where his sister Peggie and her husband, Bill, were living. Two weeks later, he got a letter from his father. He was still living in Kyushu, a testament to the fallibility of doctors and his own orneriness. Tom's brother, Frank, was living in Tokyo. Two months later, there was another letter from a relative in Japan. There would be no reunion. Tom's father had died.

●   ●   ●

WITH THE WAR BEHIND HIM, Tom had to consider his future. Barb Hinkle had married a coast guard man and moved to a tiny town in Montana. The Dirty Eight were scattered all over the Northwest, going to school, driving trucks, cutting logs. In five years, the world had grown astronomically larger, and Port Angeles had shrunk. There was no longer enough room for a young Japanese-American boy with ambition.

Much of America was not ready for the Japanese Americans, even those who returned in uniform. Prominent businesspeople and politicians in the White River and Puyallup valleys south of Seattle formed the Remember Pearl Harbor League to protest against the Japanese farmers and their families returning to their communities. The International Brotherhood of the Teamsters, the Eagles, and the American Legion were among those urging the Japanese Americans be banned from the West Coast.

Commander Melvyn McCoy, who spent eleven months in a Japanese prison camp in the Philippines, told a crowd of a thousand people attending a Seattle meeting of the Remember

Pearl Harbor League that he thought the Japanese Americans should be exiled to one of the islands captured from the Japanese.

"When the boys return from the South Pacific, I think they will tell you that the only good Jap is a dead Jap," he said.

Northwest religious leaders and academics risked their reputations and their jobs fighting for the right of the internees to return to the Puget Sound area. But when the Japanese Americans started straggling back home, they were met by hostility or indifference. Jobs advertised in the newspaper were mysteriously filled when a person with an Asian face applied. No JAPS ALLOWED signs were common in restaurants, stores, and clubs. Property and income losses suffered by Japanese Americans during the war are estimated at between $150 million and $360 million (in 1945 dollars; in 1983 dollars, the range would lie between $810 million and $2 billion).

There was nothing left for Tom in Port Angeles, so he decided to settle down in Minnesota, where he could be near Peggie and some of his military buddies. He and a friend imported fresh flowers from Seattle and sold them on the streets to pay for classes at the university. Occasionally, he heard from one of the Dirty Eight by telephone or through the mail. Shortly after he was discharged from the army, Bud Willson had caught a train east to visit him. They went to Illinois and visited Chiyono before going on to Chicago to visit another military friend. One night, Bud and Tom stayed up well past midnight sharing stories about the war—everything, that is, but the internment camps. It was like an uncomfortable piece of family history or a terminal illness, a topic to be avoided.

A few years after the war ended, Tom decided it was time to invest in a home where he and his wife, Yoshino, the sister of a friend, could raise a family. He didn't have the five thousand dollars for a down payment, and he needed it quickly. The only person he knew with that kind of cash was Bud Willson, who was working at the family hardware store back in Port Angeles. One phone call later, the money was on its way. He held on to the money for a few days but didn't like the feeling of indebtedness. So he sent it back to Willson with a thank-you note. At least he knew it was there.

In 1950, Chiyono was diagnosed with cancer. Her only wish was to see her first son, Frank, whom she hadn't seen since he was a baby. The Osasa children wrote to their brother and asked him to come to America and meet his mother. Frank wrote back, saying he would try to come as soon as he could save up enough money.

"In a country as great as America there must be a doctor that can save her," his letter said. "You have to keep her alive so I can see her once." But Chiyono died a year later, without ever seeing the son she had been forced to leave behind.

Armed with a business degree from the University of Minnesota, Tom moved to Portland, where he worked as an accountant before eventually joining the U.S. Department of Agriculture as an auditor. In 1966, he was sent to Japan to do a marketing survey for the U.S. government. It would be his first meeting with his brother Frank, whom he knew only through letters.

The man Tom saw when he got off the airplane at Haneda Airport was his brother—the resemblance was unmistakable. But growing up on the other side of the Pacific Ocean had

taken a great physical toll on Frank. Though there was just
over a year between them, it looked as if decades separated
them. Frank's hair was white, and he had only a few teeth,
the legacy of the poor nutrition after the war. He was nearly
deaf from a wartime accident. Tom, on the other hand, had a
head of coal-black hair and a suntan from his weekends on the
golf course.

Four decades earlier, Masaru Osasa had taken a gamble.
By leaving his eldest son behind in Japan, he hoped to ensure
that at least one Osasa would have the benefits of a strict
Japanese upbringing and superior education. The rest of the
family would make the sacrifices, slaving away in a hot Port
Angeles kitchen and sending money back to Japan to pay
Frank's bills. But fate didn't cooperate.

While Tom was traveling with the marines in the Philippines, his brother was on a ship somewhere in the Pacific
fighting for the Japanese Navy. When Tom was in Yokohama
helping MacArthur's staff rebuild Japan in the image of the
United States, his brother was starving in Tokyo.

Thanks to a college education subsidized by money sent
to Japan by Chiyono, Frank was able to get a job with a
company that produced labels for products made by Hitachi.
But he lived in a cramped apartment with few luxuries. Using
his privileges at the U.S. military base, Tom bought food and
electronic goods for his brother, his brother's wife, and their
three sons. He also purchased an expensive hearing aid for his
brother.

During the three months Tom spent in Japan, he learned
more about his father's life after Port Angeles. When Masaru
Osasa first returned to Japan, he moved in with Frank. But

any hopes of developing a relationship with his father were shattered by the realities of life with a bitter old man. After they parted company, the elder Osasa apparently moved back to his family's original home in Kyushu where he stayed until his death.

Frank told his brother that he wasn't sure whether their father had ever found happiness, although he apparently never stopped trying. There were other businesses, other women, and apparently other dreams.

• • •

OVER THE YEARS, Tom Osasa kept tabs on the other members of the Dirty Eight through Christmas cards, phone calls, and occasional visits. He heard about Bud Willson selling the family hardware business and Sam Haguewood's stint as mayor. Tom returned to Port Angeles several times for high-school reunions, and they would all gather at Haguewood's Restaurant and share stories about their families, their travels, and their problems.

Tom's climb up the career ladder at the Department of Agriculture kept his family—Yoshino and three children—on the move. In 1979, he retired from the position of regional inspector general with twenty-seven years of government service.

In 1989, following a long campaign led by the Japanese American Citizens League to obtain reparations for the World War II internment, then President George Bush signed a bill that set aside twenty thousand dollars each for those who were sent to the internment camps. Chiyono, like many of the first-generation internees, had already died. But Tom and his sister,

Peggie, each got a check from the government that went into their retirement accounts. Looking back on those months the Osasas spent behind the barbed wire, and considering the money they lost when they closed down their restaurant, it was tough to feel guilty about taking the money.

Sitting in his luxury condominium in Palm Desert, California, a retirement community with a fondness for pseudo-Spanish architecture, manicured greenery, and streets named after deceased Hollywood stars, Tom is several lifetimes away from his friends in Port Angeles. A government pension, some careful investing, and an occasional good hand at the tables in Las Vegas have allowed him to fulfill his teenage fantasies of the good life. He remarried after Yoshino died from cancer. His days are now organized around golf games, dinners out with his second wife, Sarah, and occasional visits from his children and grandchildren.

Tom's memories of Port Angeles are carefully filed away in old photo albums that are musty and frayed at the edges. There are photos of the Osasa children in the park in downtown Seattle; a graying picture of his father, a tall handsome man in a dark western suit; a photo of his mother and sister standing in their restaurant. In page after page, there are photos of Barb in various poses. Tucked away in the back are the photos from Tom's high-school reunions, capturing the Dirty Eight as they succumb to the passage of time; with each passing year there are less hair, bigger waistlines, and more people with bifocals. Over the years, their numbers have thinned; Ervin, Church, and Haguewood have died.

In the half-dozen times Tom returned to Port Angeles after the war, no one ever asked him a question about his father's alleged career as a spy. In fact, he is shocked to find out that the story is still floating around. But there is a lot the friends haven't talked about. Even his best friend, Bud Willson, a man who speaks his mind and pays for it, has never been able to bring himself to ask Tom about those months in the internment camp.

Willson, a slender man who looks like he was born in jeans and a flannel shirt, was one of the Dirty Eight who never really left the Olympic Peninsula. Although he lived and worked several years in Seattle and other cities, he always figured he would eventually return to his hometown. The happiest years of his working life were spent in a tugboat guiding giant cargo ships in and out of Port Angeles harbor. He married his high school sweetheart, Doris, after her first marriage fell through. The couple live in a brick rambler on the crest of a hill overlooking Port Angeles Harbor, where they raised two children.

It was April 1986, when *National Geographic*, the armchair traveler's window to the world, brought Willson into a place his best friend had never taken him. Called "Japanese Americans, Home at Last," the article told the history of Japanese immigrants, of their efforts to find a place in American society in spite of the hatred they faced, and recounted their imprisonment during World War II.

The segment about the internment camps like Tule Lake was the most troubling. The photos accompanying the article showed somber families lined up at the train station with their suitcases, the stark barracks furnished with an oil stove and light bulb, the barbed-wire fences and armed guards. In one particularly poignant letter, a young medical student, Kazuyuki Takahashi, explained how demeaning it was to depend on the government to provide toilet paper and sugar. "Sometimes I wonder whether I'm right in maintaining, somehow, faith in the American Way—or whatever you want to call it," he wrote to a former professor.

For the first time, in reading that article, Willson was forced to face the things that had been too painful for Tom to talk about: the lack of privacy, the loneliness, and worst of all, the humiliating knowledge that someone, somewhere, regards you as a traitor.

The Port Angeles native sat there in his home overlooking the harbor where he and his young Japanese-American friend used to fish and swim, and felt fifty years roll over him. It was a wave of anger, guilt, and disgust that left tears in his eyes and his heart somewhere in the pit of his stomach. He had never been so ashamed to call himself an American.

Bubbles
of Death

MORE THAN ONCE, when someone has asked about her sister, Elsye, Thelma Helgeson has been tempted to sit down and write a book. Boiled down to its essence, the story is about a family's tragic loss, an elderly Japanese woman looking for redemption, and the Japanese-American professor who brought the two sides together. It is about two nations at war and the people who suffered, about the ones who seemed compelled to look beyond their hatred and the others who wear their hatred like a badge of pride.

But hardly anything is really that simple, at least for a sixty-seven-year-old woman who has seen the Japanese go from being a bitter enemy to an economic superpower capable of buying up Los Angeles skyscrapers and Hollywood studios and even the pulp and paper mill that pays the bills for many of her neighbors.

For Thelma, memory begins with her and Elsye playing hide-and-seek in a vacant house at Camp Talbott, a logging camp outside of Port Angeles where their father worked. Elsye, who was nine, took off with the other children while Thelma found a suitable hiding place. It was hours later that a panicked Elsye and her father found the lost five-year-old. Thelma was fast asleep in a closet.

Elsye felt so guilty. She was born responsible, always looking out for others, particularly her younger sister. There were eight kids born to Oscar and Fannie Winters—five girls and three boys—and in a house with that many people the alliances were forged early on. Elsye was the more contemplative one, the one who wanted to play Sunday school when everyone else was playing house. Thelma had a kind of up-front, tell-it-all personality that she could turn on like a faucet—and sometimes forgot to turn off.

Oscar, who filed saws for loggers, followed the work, so each of the older kids was born in a different tiny logging town, towns that are just names in a scrapbook now. The logging business has always been a cyclical one. When the economy was good and people were building cities out of the wilderness, they couldn't cut down the trees on the Olympic Peninsula fast enough. But when things started to look tight and people stopped building, it was a lot cheaper to leave the trees alone. In good years, loggers and saw filers bought new cars and had a pile of presents under the Christmas tree. In bad years, they ate watered-down soup and vegetables from the garden. As the kids got older, they learned when to quit asking for something their parents couldn't afford.

When Elsye was in grade school, the Winterses moved into an old house on the site of what is now Olympic Memorial Hospital but was then a big pasture on the outskirts of Port Angeles. Money wasn't something that was talked about a lot in the Winters family, but with ten people there was never enough of it. When Laura wanted new shoes, her father went out and bought the equipment to put a half-sole on her old ones. Fannie's sewing machine was always running, and nearly every piece of clothing in the Winters family had at least two lives, sometimes three.

Their yard was a big garden filled with every kind of vegetable. Even during the Depression, before they moved to Port Angeles, Laura, the eldest daughter, never remembers being hungry. There was venison steak and salmon and milk from the cows that the Winters boys milked every morning. "Nobody in this family is going to starve, as long as there are animals in the woods and fish in the streams," Oscar would tell his family.

Fannie Winters was strict with her children, a product of the puritanical virtues preached by the Free Methodist Church. Roller skating was acceptable, and movies and makeup were not. Oscar's moral outlook wasn't as harsh. Thelma recalled sneaking into the movie house with her father a couple of times, and he made no effort to stifle his love for music, forming a band with two brothers that filled the floor at grange dances.

The news from Europe was alarming in those years, even

to the residents of an isolated timber town in the far reaches of the United States. Country after country fell to the Nazi forces, depicted in newsreels as vicious goose-stepping soldiers in total subservience to a charismatic führer.

But the threat of Hitler still felt far away from the halls of Port Angeles's Roosevelt High School. It was during those critical growing-up years—when girls discover boys and themselves—that Elsye and Thelma really became close friends.

While the Dirty Eight were going to the dance halls and playing cards, Elsye and Thelma were attending Bible classes and singing in the church choir. Tom Osasa barely remembers the dark-haired Winters girls, although Thelma was in his class in school. She remembers him, though, as a "good-looking boy" and a good athlete. But they ran in different crowds.

Irene Wagner, a high school social science teacher, encouraged Elsye to pursue her studies of the Bible and music. Both Elsye and Thelma attended Wagner's Bible study classes twice a week in the old city library. Elsye taught herself to play the piano through a correspondence course, wrote poetry, and sang in the glee club.

In one of her clearest displays of independence, Elsye changed the spelling of her name from Elsie to Elsye shortly after graduating from high school in 1939. She told people she thought it looked better with her middle name, May. But there was another motive. She shared her name with an aunt she wasn't fond of and a famous cow used to advertise Borden's milk.

By the early part of 1940, the year Elsye entered Seattle Pacific College, Hitler had taken Czechoslovakia and Poland and was amassing troops for an attack on Great Britain. Many

Americans remained hopeful that their boys would not have to enter "Europe's war." And Japan, with its invasion of China, appeared to be focusing its attention on its Asian neighbors. The danger from that side of the world seemed of far less concern than the battles being fought in Europe.

Of course, that changed on December 7, 1941. Within a few weeks, it felt as if the entire population of Port Angeles had been drafted into the war: able-bodied men recruited to patrol the ocean beaches; young women called upon to serve as dance partners at the weekly dances in the basement of the USO hall; housewives asked to enlist in exercise programs to get their bodies into better shape in case they were called upon.

As a high school student, Thelma had more on her mind than geopolitics. There were a lot of handsome young men hanging around downtown, men from places in America of which locals had never heard, men with southern drawls and Brooklyn accents and sweet smiles. But while a lot of her friends got involved with the soldiers—and more than a few of them ended up pregnant—Thelma was on a tight leash. Her mother didn't let her daughters go to any dance halls, movie theaters, or bars. For the Winters girls, a walk on the wild side was an evening at the skating rink.

After attending Seattle Pacific College for one year, Elsye transferred to Simpson Bible Institute in Seattle. When Thelma graduated in 1942, she followed her sister to Seattle, and they roomed together at the dormitory and sang in the choir.

Elsye graduated in 1943 but not before meeting her future husband, Archie Mitchell, an Ellensburg boy who was on his way to becoming an ordained minister. In August, Elsye and Archie were married in Port Angeles and spent their honeymoon driving to Nyack, New York, where they enrolled in a school affiliated with the Christian Missionary Alliance. Never as drawn to church work as her sister, Thelma lost interest in Bible studies after Elsye left. With the war on, and money tighter, Thelma decided to move home and get a job.

Separated for the first time, the Winters girls kept track of each other's comings and goings by mail, with regular updates on Elsye's Bible school classes, Thelma's dating, and the news from the war. It was the only hope of staying in touch with the incremental steps in each other's increasingly disparate lives.

After leaving New York, Archie and Elsye Mitchell went to work at a church in Ellensburg, a small eastern Washington town surrounded by cattle ranches. Elsye took up writing and was working on a story called "Cabin in the Hills" when a parsonage fire destroyed her typewriter and her early attempt at a literary career.

In the spring of 1945, the Mitchells were given a chance to go out on their own. The tiny timber town of Bly, Oregon, population 750, seemed like a good place for a young pastor and his wife. The Christian Missionary Alliance Church of Bly was more than just a place to worship the creator. It was a center around which spun the dinners and children's outings and friendships that were the high society of small-town America. The Mitchells packed up their car and headed for Bly. After the flat, dry terrain of eastern Washington, they were looking forward to some hiking and fishing in the pine forests. Building up their church wasn't going to be easy, especially since the Pentecostals had moved to town. But across the Pacific Ocean, the feeling was one of much greater desperation.

•　　•　　•

Though it may not mean going to the battlefield, all must participate in this just war to protect the emperor. Girls, you too go in earnest, go with pride.

Reiko Okada remembers those words clearly, the call to arms that were used to inspire the young women of Tadanoumi Girls' High School in the fall of 1944.

She was just thirteen years old, the age when girls in Japan should have been learning drama and playing sports instead of memorizing the right way to seal a smoke canister and the proper method for making a deadly paper balloon.

She was also about the same age as Dick and Joan Patzke, Jay Gifford, Eddie Engen, and Sherman Shoemaker, five American children whom she would only know as names on a tombstone decades later.

But Japan was fighting the war of its life, the divine race against the white barbarians, the soldiers of Yamato defending their culture of 2,600 years against the foreign devils. The great Pacific war demanded everyone serve as its soldiers, a universal draft that started and ended with the national borders of the island archipelago. Even Okinawa, an island that had fought Japanese rule, was enlisted in the fight against the Western oppressors.

Collecting paper, conserving water, or marching in victory parades were all part of the cause, and the national mood was one of euphoria during the early months of the war when the Japanese soldiers marched across Asia claiming beach after beach, city after city, as their own. But as the war dragged on, and the Rising Sun fell more often to the Allied forces, the Japanese government grew desperate. In 1942—stunned by Colonel Jimmy Doolittle's surprise air attack on Tokyo, Yokohama, Nagoya, and Kobe—the Japanese government started working on secret weapons.

The Fu-Go project, as it was called, was the Japanese government's effort to harness the high-altitude air currents that flow across the Pacific Ocean at speeds of up to three hundred miles per hour. As far back as 1933, the Japanese government had begun researching the use of balloons to carry explosive devices into enemy territory.

It took two years to develop an unmanned hydrogen-filled silk or paper balloon capable of staying aloft across thousands of miles of ocean. The balloons were designed to float to a certain altitude and catch the current of air across the Pacific. When it reached the west coast of North America, using an elaborate system of ballast and altitude controls, the balloon was rigged to drop the explosives.

A prisoner of the weather, the Fu-Go project could only operate between November and March, when the wind currents across the Pacific were at their strongest. Launchings could only take place on cloudless days with little surface wind, since balloons caught in the rain or snow would accumulate moisture that would freeze and add weight. In that five-month window, the Japanese military figured there would only be fifty days available for launching and a maximum of two hundred balloons a day could be set afloat from any of the three major launch sites on the eastern coast of Honshu.

The date for the initial launching was set for November 3, 1944, the birthday of Emperor Meiji, the great-great-grandfather of the emperor then reigning. To produce the thousands of handmade balloons needed by that deadline would require a massive mobilization of human energy. The Japanese government turned to the only people who weren't old, weak, or already fighting.

It was thirteen-year-old Reiko Okada and the rest of the emperor's children who were selected to turn one of Japan's ancient art forms into beautiful bubbles of death. Across the country, thousands of high school girls, chosen for their dexterity, began receiving their orders to join the nation's war against the Western imperialists.

In a book written by Okada entitled *Ohkuno Island: Story of the Student Brigade*, she tells of being called to duty at the Ohkuno Island Toxic Gas Factory with the rest of her class of thirteen-year-olds. The small island, which lies a few miles off the coast in Japan's Inland Sea, never appeared on Japanese maps because it had been a major site for chemical weapons manufacturing since 1929. Curtains were drawn on the trains that ran along the coastline and in the ferry boats that serviced the islands off the coast. During World War II, up to five thousand people, including factory workers, clerical staff, members of the young women's volunteer corps, and students, made the pilgrimage to the island.

Every morning, clothed in baggy trousers, white headbands, and battle jackets made of old kimonos, Okada and her friends, who lived in the town of Tadanoumi, boarded a ferry for the island. The first day, the plant director told the group they would be working on a top-secret project. They were warned to take nothing from the plant and were inspected every night before leaving.

Their first job was making smoke canisters, which were

filled with chemicals and ignition powder and sealed with thin layers of tin. After that, Okada and the others were put to work making the paper for the balloon bombs. Using a thick root paste called *konnyaku-nori*, they would layer five pieces of thin paper on a revolving metal box. The pieces would be peeled off the box and placed on a glass box with a light inside so they could be checked for weak spots or tears. Any defects were marked with a red pencil, reinforced with paper, moistened with caustic soda and washed with water.

From there, the paper was boiled in glycerin to produce a thin, very resilient bluish paper. The paper would again be checked for holes; repairs would be made using paper patches and more *konnyaku-nori*. The final product was cut into triangular shapes of descending sizes and pasted together into strips about eight meters long.

During the cool fall mornings, the temperature inside the building would drop so low Okada felt like she was rubbing ice, instead of paste, into the paper. But she tried hard not to slow down for fear of being reprimanded by the supervising officer. At three P.M., the girls would take a break. Over the loudspeaker, an announcer would broadcast military music and report on the latest war victory. Large salty rice balls and a cup of tea, wartime delicacies, were handed out. Food was so scarce that some of them would save their rice balls for their brothers or sisters back at home.

After the break, the young girls would return to work. The long triangular paper strips were laid out on the floor, forming a giant hemisphere, each piece overlapping for strength. Then, two hemispheres would be attached at the middle to form a ball.

A curtain of fringe was attached to each balloon for carrying the bombs. The balloon was inflated, and the girls were sent inside with flashlights to check for holes. When the balloon was finished, two dozen girls armed with paintbrushes and pails would line up and cover the outside with waterproof lacquer. The completed balloon was packed in a box for travel to another factory where the bombs were attached.

When Okada first learned of the balloon project, she was pleased that "a pilot doesn't have to die" in pursuit of another war trophy. But there wasn't a lot of time to dwell on the fate of the balloons, not in a country whose future was looking bleaker with each field report. After the loss of Saipan and the fall of Okinawa, the Japanese government finally began publicly admitting what its military leaders had privately accepted many months earlier: The powerful U.S. forces were winning island after island, atoll after atoll, and getting closer to the Japanese islands.

If Japan was attacked, the military feared Ohkuno Island might explode in a deadly cloud of toxic gases. Protecting their country now became a matter of dismantling what they had worked so hard to build. Day after day, often without anything but rubber gloves and maybe a mask, Okada and her friends tore down walls, mopped up chemical spills, and loaded drums of leaking chemicals onto ferryboats for removal to a more secure storage area. Years later, when Okada would hear reports of former classmates suffering from cancer, she would think back on the fumes they breathed from those spilled barrels.

But it was death at the hands of the American GI's that was the greatest fear for the Japanese. Okada and her classmates even cut down the pine trees and dug up the roots so they could extract oil to use as fuel for the fighter planes.

Japan's Mitsubishi Zeros were no match for the American's secret weapon, the nuclear bomb being created in the deserts of New Mexico. On August 6, 1945, just after eight A.M., three B-29's appeared in the sky above Hiroshima. The lead plane, the *Enola Gay*, dropped the atomic bomb that instantly killed close to a hundred thousand people. Thousands more died later of burns, shock, or radiation poisoning. Three days later, a second B-29 made a pass over Kokura, the home of one balloon-bomb factory, but the cloud cover was too thick. That bomber was diverted to Nagasaki, the port city that was once the only place where foreigners were allowed to live during the period when Japan was closed off to the rest of the world. Nearly thirty-five thousand more Japanese died in the second explosion.

At noon on August 15, the voice of Emperor Hirohito, the son of heaven, was heard in living rooms and schools and military bases all across Japan. And when he was finished talking, in that unmistakable ancient vernacular reserved only for the one who is a direct descendant of the Sun Goddess, he had set his children free:

> *Unite your total strength to be devoted to the construction of the future. Cultivate the ways of rectitude; foster nobility of spirit; and work with resolution as you may enhance the innate glory of the Imperial State and keep pace with the progress of the world.*

•   •   •

WHEN ALL THE ABLE-BODIED MEN in Port Angeles went off to fight the war in Europe and the Pacific, Thelma and her friends found themselves doing things they had never thought were possible. For the first time in Port Angeles history, there was a woman delivering mail, women working at the shipyards on the site of the former Michael Earles/Charles Nelson mill, women in the two big pulp and paper mills that anchor the Port Angeles waterfront. Women were bringing home paychecks and holding down jobs previously reserved for men.

During 1944 and 1945, Thelma worked on the eastern end of the harbor at the pulp mill owned by ITT Rayonier, the Northwest timber giant. She was in the finishing department, the last stop for the rolls of pulp that started out as wood chips and ended up as paper, film, and fabric. Her responsibility was a hunk of metal nicknamed the flying machine that wrapped brown paper around the rolls as they came off the end of the line. It was tough work, hour after hour of wrapping, crimping, and getting ready to take on the next roll. Those were the days when people did most of the heavy work.

One of the toughest parts of working at a pulp and paper mill is the shift work. Day shift, swing shift, graveyard. About three days into a shift, the body clock would start to adjust and then it would be racheted forward. Thelma would come home from work so tired that every bone in her body, every muscle, every tendon, was in pain. If she were lucky, there would be a letter from Elsye filled with chatty tidbits about life with Archie, the responsibilities of being a minister's wife, and, in the spring of 1945, the giddiness of becoming a mother. Elsye was pregnant, nearly five months along. Sometimes, Thelma couldn't help feeling just a little bit jealous of her older sister's life—the independence and excitement. It all seemed so perfect.

On May 5, 1945, three months and a day before America would drop the bomb on Hiroshima, Thelma was working swing shift. When the whistle blew marking the end of her shift, she was a mass of sore muscles. By the time a friend dropped her off in the alley outside her house, it was well after midnight. The lanky twenty-one-year-old walked into the house, past her mother's bedroom, and stopped. The combination of the light being on and the lack of movement told her something was wrong.

She went into the room and her mother was sitting in bed, just staring at nothing, her brown eyes wide open, her Bible lying on top of the covers. Her mother said, "I have some news for you. Archie Mitchell called and said Elsye was killed."

Elsye was killed. Three little words and a piece of Thelma just shriveled up and died. There would be no more warnings about waiting for the right guy, no more late-night giggling, no more speculation about what Elsye was going to name that little baby she was expecting in five months. And Archie, Elsye's husband, couldn't even tell them how she died, just that there was a terrible accident.

In a crisis, when a human being is trying to do anything not to fall apart, information is critical; lack of it becomes a black hole filled with the worst possibilities. There were tears. There was anger. There was even speculation by a not-so-distant relative that Archie, that earnest young man of the cloth, had killed his twenty-six-year-old pregnant wife.

Two days later, there was a story in the *Port Angeles Evening News* that Elsye and five children had been killed in an unidentified explosion in the mountains near Lakeview, Oregon. The rumors escalated. Anytime the family left the house, there were people waiting to put their own spin on the tragedy. For several days, Thelma didn't go to work. There were too many people outside the safety of the Winterses' home, people who wanted answers that nobody had. It was two long weeks before Archie arrived at the Winterses' front door and told them how Elsye had died.

On the morning of May 4, just a couple of weeks after their move from Ellensburg to Oregon, Elsye was feeling pretty good. She hadn't had a bad bout of morning sickness for three days, and now had enough energy to clean the house and bake a chocolate cake. That would be her contribution to tomorrow's picnic. Archie wanted to take some of his Sunday school kids out for a day in the woods.

She took some time to write a letter to Thelma.

"They wanted me to go along but since I'm still pretty weak I won't be able to keep up with a bunch of boys," she wrote. "They wouldn't have any fun with an old woman in my circumstances tagging along. One of the guys who is down here a lot, Dick Patzke, just couldn't understand why I was sick so much. He was telling me all kinds of things to take and I just laughed up my sleeve. He's almost 16. I just about up and told him but thought I wouldn't. He would find out soon enough."

The next morning, Elsye changed her mind. Perhaps it was the good weather—the sky was blue, even though there was still snow on Gearhart Mountain. Or maybe it was just not wanting to disappoint her husband and that silly Dick Patzke.

Dick, a big kid with a mop of unruly hair and a grin that stole half his face, brought along his fishing pole in case they happened to stumble across a trout stream in their search for the perfect picnic spot. Also along were his thirteen-year-old sister, Joan; Jay Gifford and Eddie Engen, also thirteen; and eleven-year-old Sherman Shoemaker.

They all piled into the Mitchells' sixteen-year-old sedan and drove east out of Bly for a mile before turning north onto a U.S. Forest Service road that headed into a forest of junipers, pine, and fir. The road eventually wound its way up the south side of Gearhart Mountain into a pine forest owned by Weyerhaeuser Timber Co.

Shortly before the road crosses Leonard Creek, Archie stopped. A U.S. Forest Service crew was wrestling with a road grader in the middle of the narrow road. Elsye and the kids climbed out and wandered toward the creek while Archie looked for a place to park the car.

They could easily have walked right past that cylindrical metal object, half buried in the underbrush. Others probably had, since it had been there for some time, judging from the rusted metal edges and the mildew on the paper balloon. No one is sure what happened next, although most suspect it was one of the children, curious to the last moment, who triggered the fifteen-kilogram high-explosive bomb.

"Look what I found, dear" were the last words Archie heard from his wife as he ran through the woods toward the group.

Gearhart Mountain exploded. Trees were blown apart, pine needles fell like rain, and the earth shook. Archie and two U.S. Forest Service employees who had been working on the road nearby raced toward the blast. Archie reached Elsye and began beating out the flames that were devouring her clothes, but she and all five children died within minutes. His hands were stained bright yellow from the acid contained in the explosive package.

The tragedy of five families was a national military emergency. That evening, a somber group of uniformed officers delivered the news to the Patzkes, the Engens, the Shoemakers, the Giffords, and Archie Mitchell with a request that they not say anything to anyone. Archie made his cryptic phone call to the Winterses' home in Port Angeles. For the time being, those six deaths were classified information.

The U.S. government had suspected for months that the Japanese had embarked on a campaign to recruit nature into its secret arsenal of war weapons. A deflated rubberized silk balloon was discovered floating in the Pacific Ocean off the coast of California in November 1944; a second balloon fragment was recovered two weeks later in the sea near Kailua, Hawaii. Another balloon was reported near Kalispell, Montana, on December 11, and eight days later a bomb crater was discovered near Thermopolis, Wyoming. By the end of 1944, eight balloon incidents had been reported on the West Coast.

By mid-January, the U.S. government was confident it knew what the bombs were and from where in Japan they were being launched. Project Sunset was the code name given to the army's campaign to defend the country from the balloon bombs. Ten radar units along the Washington coast were put on twenty-four-hour alert. Weather stations were used to provide information about the probable courses of incoming balloons.

At first, the greatest fear was that the bombs would explode in the mountains and start forest fires, prompting the movement of 2,700 troops, including 200 paratroopers, to stand ready to fight forest fires in potentially hazardous areas thoughout the West Coast. Then, the possibility was raised that the bombs might be carrying some form of deadly chemicals or germs. The Lightning Project was organized through the Department of Agriculture: Word was spread to veterinarians, 4-H Clubs, and others on the farm circuit to be on the lookout for strange behavior in cows or other livestock. Decontamination sprays were quietly distributed throughout the West.

Aircraft were frequently dispatched to try to bring down the balloons that were sighted, but they proved to be wily opponents and only two were ever shot down over the North American continent. A balloon was chased by fighter planes all the way from Redmond, Oregon, into Nevada before starting its descent in the mountains near Reno. One determined pilot landed his plane and continued the chase by automobile but the balloon dropped some of its load and took off again. The balloon was finally brought down by gunfire from one of three planes still in the air.

The U.S. government's own secret-weapon program was endangered briefly when a wayward balloon hit a power line serving the nuclear plant at Hanford, Washington, where researchers were racing to produce the materials needed to build the atomic bombs later dropped over Japan. The Hanford blackout triggered the nuclear reactor's safety mechanism and shut down the plant for three days.

The cause of the blackout was not reported to the public, however, because the U.S. military didn't want the Japanese government to know its secret campaign was working. On January 4, 1945, the U.S. censorship office ordered newspaper editors and radio broadcasters not to publicize the existence of the balloon bombs. It worked. The only incident that received widespread media coverage was the discovery of the bomb crater in Wyoming, which was reported by a Chinese newspaper and made its way back to Japanese officials.

In February, the Japanese government launched an unsuccessful effort to jeopardize the U.S. government's censorship campaign by releasing its own information. In English-language radio broadcasts directed at the United States, and later beamed to Europe, China, and Southeast Asia, the Japanese claimed that the balloon bombs had inflicted between five hundred and ten thousand casualties and caused numerous fires. Apparently little attention was paid to the obvious propaganda broadcasts.

The explosion on Gearhart Mountain ended the government's gag order. On May 31, the army and navy issued a joint statement about the Japanese balloon-bomb campaign that ran on the front page of newspapers from coast to coast: "It is desirable that people and especially children living west of the Mississippi River be warned of this possible hazard and cautioned under no circumstances to touch or approach any unfamiliar object." Also, the statement went on, the "possibility of saving even one American life through precautionary measures would more than offset any military gain which the enemy might make from the mere knowledge that some of the balloons had arrived on this side of the Pacific."

By that time, the Japanese government, frustrated by the expense and apparent lack of success, had discontinued the campaign. Only a small percentage of the nine thousand balloons that were launched reached North America. The two hundred eighty-five fragments of bombs or balloons that were recovered had floated as far north as the island of Attu in the Aleutians, as far east as Michigan, and as far south as Mexico. It was considered lucky—in fact a miracle—that the only casualties of the Japanese balloon-bomb campaign—in fact, the only deaths of civilians on the U.S. mainland during World War II—were Elsye and the five children.

In a 1950 article in *Reader's Digest*, retired brigadier general W. H. Wilbur, Chief of Staff of the Western Defense Command, called the balloons a "significant development in the art of war" because potentially dangerous missiles were successfully sent overseas without human guidance. He said the devastation could have been tremendous if the balloons had been equipped with bacteriological agents or hundreds of small incendiaries instead of a few large ones. He also said it was the news blackout that persuaded the Japanese to give up the campaign.

But in her grief over Elsye's death, Laura Jo Whipple, the eldest of the five sisters, couldn't forgive the U.S. government or the media for failing to warn the public as soon as they knew of the danger.

A month after the explosion, Laura, who was living with her husband in Seattle, wrote Elmer Todd, publisher of the *Seattle Times*, and asked why the newspaper had not printed the information that could have saved her younger sister's life. A week later, she received a letter in which Todd expressed his regret that the U.S. government had censored the reports on the Japanese balloon bombs. "I agree with you that it was a mistake for the O.W.I. [Office of War Instruction] to conceal the facts about these Japanese balloons for so many months," the publisher wrote. "The newspapers knew about them but were forbidden by the government to publish anything about them. Since then, we have published everything that the U.S. government and other authorities have furnished us. I do not know how we can do anything more because there are no further facts being furnished us."

There was an effort, years later, to try to make amends. In May 1949, Congress passed legislation granting five thousand dollars to Archie Mitchell and three thousand dollars to the parents of each of the children.

Elsye was buried at Ocean View Cemetery on a bone-chilling Port Angeles day. Eva, who was sixteen at the time, couldn't stop crying. There was something so wrong about her sister, the one who had always been right up there next to the angels, being buried on a day like this.

"The thought of her being put in the ground just tore me up something awful," said the youngest of the sisters, who was living at home with Thelma and their parents. "It was so final."

•   •   •

A COUPLE OF WEEKS AFTER Elsye's funeral, Thelma climbed on a bus headed for Ellensburg and met up with Elsye's husband, Archie, for the long drive back to Bly. She was the one chosen to go through Elsye's things. Thelma remembers how the most mundane things took on a whole new importance. It was as if someone had taken a snapshot that caught the perfect family in that moment before disaster struck. Inside the tiny bungalow where Archie and Elsye lived, a laundry basket sat on the kitchen table filled with clean clothes waiting to be folded. Next to the basket were some flannel baby kimonos, some patterns for baby clothes, and a piece of old material waiting for a new life.

And then there was the canned pineapple. By the end of the war, rationing had become a way of life; there were many things that you just did without. But in the kitchen cupboard there was a can Elsye had been saving to make her favorite pineapple upside-down cake to celebrate the visit of her best friends, Nathan and Helen Ost. That can of pineapple just seemed like it held a lifetime of missed opportunities.

Bly was a town imploding with anger and hurt. The loss of five children, and the pastor's wife, was just too much pain to impose on a couple of blocks of loggers and their families. But Thelma managed to hold back her tears through those long days with the grieving husband and bereaved relatives.

Her grief finally caught up with her on the long bus ride back to Port Angeles. Thelma needed Elsye's advice on a problem, one she had been wrestling with for weeks. She had started dating a man from work who had come to fix her machine when it broke down. He was a wrestler in his spare time and a bouncer at the local dance hall. He was also divorced with two kids.

Oscar and Fannie weren't too sure about bringing this Archie, Archie Helgeson, into their family. In the Winterses' eyes, he was an older man who had already had enough excitement for at least one, maybe two, lifetimes. But Thelma wished her parents could see the sweet guy who—when confronted with a woman who didn't drink, dance, or go to movies—drove out to a lake and rented a rowboat on their first date.

It was kind of eerie. Thelma hadn't gotten a chance to tell her sister about her new boyfriend. But in Elsye's last letter, which was delivered on the day she was killed, it was as if she had read Thelma's mind. "Are you still not going with any male?" Elsye wrote. "You have lots of time to be unattached, and better always that way than with the wrong man. It must be an awful feeling to wake up to the fact that you have married the wrong man. Most folks just don't think straight beforehand or won't listen to what others say—but the marriage union is too sacred to be entered blindly. I still say I have the best husband there is."

When Thelma arrived in Port Angeles, Archie Helgeson was there to meet her. And in the grim months after Elsye's death, he was the only one who could make her laugh. That September, Thelma and Archie were married in the Free Methodist Church while Oscar sat in a front-row pew. Tom, the eldest Winters boy, gave Thelma away. Oscar said he couldn't walk down that aisle so soon after marrying off Elsye.

There was another noticeable absence at that wedding. Archie Mitchell, who had returned to his job in Bly, sent the newlyweds a package and a letter in which he explained that he couldn't bring himself to visit the church where he had been married just two years and twelve days earlier.

In the package Archie sent were some of Elsye's things, including a worn cookbook, the *Searchlight Recipe Book*, that Thelma still uses. "I couldn't send them to anyone else and I know you will appreciate them even if they aren't exactly new," the widower wrote. "They are better than new because they belonged to Elsye."

Five years later, Archie Mitchell married Betty Patzke, the

elder sister of the two children killed in the explosion. Thelma, preoccupied with the responsibilities of caring for her aging parents and raising Helgeson's two young children, who were five and eight years old at the time of the marriage, eventually lost touch with her former brother-in-law.

In 1962, Thelma got a phone call from one of her siblings. Had she heard the news about Archie? Since 1950, he and Betty had been running a Christian Missionary Alliance leprosarium in Ban Me Thuot, a South Vietnamese city surrounded by lush coffee plantations and jungle. When the Communists seized the city, the Mitchells were among ten foreigners captured and thrown in jail. When the North Vietnamese finally released their captives eight months later, there were three who didn't return: Dr. Eleanor A. Vietti, Daniel A. Gerber, and Archie Mitchell.

God had intervened again, but this time it was Archie who left behind a grieving spouse and a young daughter. He became one of thousands of Americans unaccounted for in the Vietnam War, whose ghosts would haunt their survivors and the two countries for decades after the fighting stopped.

•   •   •

September 10, 1987

Dear Mr. and Mrs. Helgeson,

Dottie McGinnis of Klamath Falls gave me your name and address at my request. I wanted to write to someone related to Mrs. Elsie [sic] Mitchell who suffered an untimely death some 42 years ago in the mountains of Bly, Oregon, a victim with five children of a balloon bomb that was sent across the Pacific from Japan. . . .

When Thelma opened up the letter from John Takeshita, a University of Michigan professor, it was as if Elsye had reached out across five decades and rewritten the ending to her own story.

At least once every couple of years, one of the Winters children would get a call from a newspaper reporter or maybe a letter from someone researching World War II who was interested in finding out more about the balloon-bomb incident. But the letter from Takeshita was different, born out of a series of occurrences—some might say coincidences—that spanned fifty years and thousands of miles.

Takeshita, whose Japanese first name was Yuzuru, and his brother, the sons of a California shop owner, lived in Japan from 1934 to 1940, two of the *kibei* sent back to Japan for an education. They lived with their grandfather in Yamegun, a village in southwestern Kyushu that had been turned into a temporary training center for the army. In the months before Pearl Harbor, when war seemed like a very real possibility, the two Takeshita boys were sent home to California.

In the spring of 1942, the Takeshita family was relocated to the Tule Lake relocation center, the camp in northern California where Tom Osasa's family was sent. The families don't recall meeting each other, which wouldn't be unusual in a camp of sixteen thousand people. There were rivalries between the internees from California and Washington, who were in the minority, and the two groups kept to their own neighborhoods. The *kibei*, with their accents and formal mannerisms, also met with suspicion from young Japanese Americans who knew nothing but American life.

About a year later, the rumors started going around camp

that the Japanese were floating balloon bombs across the ocean. Takeshita stood outside his barracks, squinting up into the desert sky across the border from Bly, looking for Japan's secret weapon. He never saw one.

After the war, Takeshita went to college and eventually joined the faculty at the University of Michigan as a professor of population planning and public health. In 1985, Takeshita traveled to Japan on a business trip and stopped in to see one of his best friends from elementary school.

During that visit, Toshiko Inouye, the wife of his elementary-school classmate, told him that she was one of the girls drafted by the Japanese government to build the balloon bombs that were used during World War II. Inouye told Takeshita she had heard there was a balloon on display at the Smithsonian Institution's National Air and Space Museum and asked him to take a picture of it if he ever visited the exhibit.

A year later, when Takeshita was in Washington, D.C., for a meeting, he slipped away (during a break) to the National Air and Space Museum. There was no display of a balloon, but there was a photo showing the balloons floating above the Pacific Ocean. Intrigued by this reference to the past, Takeshita read the brief description of the balloon campaign. Then he got to the part about the young pregnant woman and the five children killed in a bomb blast near Bly, Oregon.

Takeshita was shocked. He had never heard anything about the explosion on Gearhart Mountain—and his friend's wife Inouye hadn't mentioned it. When he wrote her, he enclosed the photo of the balloon-bomb display and asked that she pray for the souls of the victims.

In the fall of 1986, Takeshita returned to Japan for a year

to teach at a private university in Kobe. As the anniversary of the bombing of Hiroshima and Nagasaki approached, the television screen and newspapers were filled with stories about the tragedy of the atomic bombs. One day, he switched on the television and saw an elderly woman talking about her experience in the war as a supervisor of a group of high-school girls who were building balloons for the balloon bombs. She said she felt guilty because the working conditions were so terrible and some of the girls fell ill. Then, she said the words that made Takeshita's stomach start to churn. "Fortunately, only six people died. . . ."

Elsye and the five children had been reduced to a number.

As Takeshita continued to read and listen to the Japanese media coverage of the atomic-bomb anniversary, he began to get more angry. The focus was always on the suffering of the Japanese people, the radiation sickness, the genetic deformities, the starvation, the war casualties. "What about the innocent civilians in Nanjing and South Korea and the Philippines?" he wanted to scream at the television screen. "What about those six innocent victims?"

Two months later, Takeshita was in the city of Yamaguchi for a sociology conference on the problems of an aging society. On the last day of the conference, he was sitting in the audience waiting for the session to begin when a group of elderly women came in and sat in front of him.

He knew one of the faces, but he just couldn't place it. And then, as the hours went by, he finally remembered. The elderly woman sitting in front of him was the one who had appeared on the television program about the balloon bombs. Afterward, he went up to her and introduced himself. They exchanged name cards. Her name was Yoshiko Hisaga, a retired teacher from Yamaguchi Girls' High School.

Takeshita couldn't put the chance meeting out of his mind. When he returned to Kobe, he found a book called *The Road to Nanking* (Nanking is now more commonly romanized as Nanjing) by a Japanese reporter who had gone to China and retraced the tracks of the Japanese forces as they began their six-week campaign of genocide.

This was more than just history for Takeshita. During his stay in Japan as a young boy, he and his classmates were fed a steady diet of military propaganda about Japan's campaign to free Asia from the Western imperialists. He remembered walking around Yamegun at night in a lantern parade celebrating the fall of Nanking, only to discover much later that more than two hundred thousand men, women, and children were massacred by Japanese troops following the occupation of the southern Chinese city.

Takeshita mailed Hisaga a copy of *The Road to Nanking.* In his letter, he told her he admired her efforts to publicize the horrible impact of the war on the Japanese. But he asked if she would consider, when discussing the balloon bomb, also to offer a prayer for the six victims of the explosion on Gearhart Mountain. And he included the names and ages of Elsye and the five children copied from the small memo pad that he had carried into the Smithsonian Institution.

Four months went by. Takeshita was getting ready to leave Japan, and he started having feelings of remorse for sending that letter. Maybe he was too forward, too American. Perhaps he should apologize. Then, he got a phone call from Hisaga. She said she and her students had been so moved by his letter that they had gotten together and folded one thousand paper cranes, a symbol of good luck for the families of the victims of the Bly explosion. Would he be the go-between and deliver them to relatives of the bomb blast victims?

In June 1987, Takeshita stopped in to visit with Hisaga and her students on his way to a memorial service for his grandmother in Kyushu. Over tea and crackers, the women told him how that book and his letter had affected their lives. For years, they had seen their role as a champion of the victims of World War II. Now, it was as if they were looking into the same room from a different window. What they saw was themselves as victimizers as well as victims.

Takeshita agreed to take the thousand cranes and a letter from the women of Yamaguchi. It didn't make sense to go all the way home to Michigan and then return to the West Coast, carrying the fragile *origami* cranes and correspondence from Japan. When Takeshita arrived at his father-in-law's home in Los Angeles, he got on the telephone and ended up locating Ed Patzke, the eldest brother of Dick and Joan. Ed, whose home had become a frequent stop for visitors to the Bly monument, agreed to meet Takeshita and gave him the number of his sister, Dottie Patzke McGinnis, in Klamath Falls.

Takeshita also decided this story should be shared with others. So he got hold of several television and newspaper reporters who agreed to meet him in Bly, Oregon, at the monument to the bomb-blast victims.

Takeshita, his wife, Sun, and his daughter, Junko, drove up the California coast, taking a short side trip to visit the memorial at Tule Lake. At the Patzkes' house, they were met by reporters who accompanied the tiny caravan on the winding road up Gearhart Mountain to the spot where the explosion occurred. On August 20, 1950, Weyerhaeuser Timber Co., which owned the pine forests where the accident took place, had erected a monument to the bomb-blast victims. Junko, who was about the same age as the children killed in the accident, placed some flowers in front of the monument along with the colorful paper cranes. Then Takeshita read from the letter of Tetsuko Tanaka, one of the women who had helped build the balloons.

> *After the defeat we were told that only some of the balloons reached the United States and were useless as weapons, having caused but a few forest fires.*
>
> *Then, forty years after the war, we learned for the first time about what is known as The Oregon Tragedy, involving the loss of six lives. We who at the time were schoolgirls only sixteen years of age were nevertheless full participants in the war, bringing pain and hardship to others. Such a realization truly sent a chill down my spine.*

During that trip, Dottie McGinnis gave Takeshita the names and addresses of all the rest of the victims' surviving family members, including Thelma, Laura, and Eva. He sent them a letter and enclosed copies of the letters from Japan along with his own expression of sympathy for the family tragedy.

> *My wife, Sun, our daughter, Junko [age 10], and I were happy to serve as the intermediary on behalf of the Japanese women in their effort to seek forgiveness from you who suffered*

irreplaceable losses in the death of your loved ones. They are
painfully aware that they are asking for forgiveness for what
is unforgiveable.

Two months later, Thelma received a box in the mail from
Dottie McGinnis. Inside was a colorful wreath made from a
hundred of the intricately folded paper cranes. McGinnis had
taken the thousand paper cranes and divided them up so they
could be shared by members of the victims' families.

Over the next three years, the reconciliation of the women
from Japan and the victims of Bly would become a personal
campaign for Takeshita. A year later, at his suggestion, the
women from Yamaguchi sent a pair of Ouchi dolls, a traditional
Japanese artwork, to the Klamath Falls County Museum,
where there is a display on the balloon bomb.

On November 9, 1990, Takeshita acted as an interpreter
for a Japanese film crew that was producing a documentary on
the balloon bombs. After his first visit to Bly—which was
reported by the media in the United States and Japan—Takeshita had been contacted by Reiko Okada, who had sent him
several copies of her book on the Ohkuno Island balloon-bomb
campaign. He presented those to Ed and Opal Patzke; Dottie
McGinnis; and Eva Fowler, Elsye's younger sister, who had
come down for the ceremony from Tonasket, Washington,
with her husband, her two sons, and a grandson. A copy of
Ohkuno Island: Story of the Student Brigade was also mailed to
Thelma.

Thelma cried the first time she read Okada's book, which
portrays the balloon-bomb campaign through the eyes of a
thirteen-year-old. For just a moment, it all seemed so clear

and so sad. They were all victims—Okada, Elsye, John, and even Thelma. How could she not forgive someone like Okada, a mere child caught up in an adults' war.

At least once a year, Takeshita sends a letter to Thelma and her sisters updating them on the latest news from Bly. On December 8, 1990, the documentary on the balloon bombs aired in Japan. Hisaga, the Japanese teacher, was interviewed in the film discussing the inhumane working conditions at Kokura, one of many balloon-manufacturing sites where the young girls worked sixteen-hour days.

"I could not feed the students or could not let them sleep until we could go back to the rest house," she told the Japanese television crew. "So I tried to make them work faster and harder so that they could go back to sleep. Every time the students almost finished up one balloon, I brought them more materials for more balloons. They looked up at me as if they begged me for something or as if they hated me without saying anything, but they took the materials and went back to work."

After the documentary aired, Takeshita contacted an elementary school in Yamaguchi and the students mailed a thousand cranes to the only elementary school in Bly. The children of Bly responded by folding paper swans and sending them back to Japan.

Each new episode became a link in the bridge that has turned the balloon bombs from a personal tragedy into a testament to grass-roots diplomacy. With each addition of a letter or newspaper clipping, the Elsye files get a little bit thicker. Eva and Laura own videotaped copies of the Japanese documentary. Laura Jo has the black scrapbook given to each family after the dedication of the Mitchell Recreation Area by the

Weyerhaeuser Timber Co. on August 20, 1950. Thelma has Elsye's last letter home, a yellowing piece of paper filled with bitter ironies.

At least once or twice, after a particularly long day of emotional revelations, Thelma has told her two surviving sisters her wish that, after nearly fifty years of reliving the tragedy and discussing its consequences, she could just bury her sister once and for all. Elsye was, and always will be, an important part of Thelma's life. But sometimes, her elevation to a symbol of cross-cultural understanding has been an intrusion. Instead of being allowed to mourn her death in private, and share Elsye's life with those who knew her, Thelma feels she is at the mercy of outsiders who want feelings expressed on their schedules.

Thelma doesn't expect, or want, to forget her sister. She just wants to be able, at some level, to remember her without the public scrutiny. Every Memorial Day, Thelma goes up to Ocean View Cemetery with a metal can filled with flowers from her garden. At Elsye's grave, there is a simple gravestone purchased by the American Legion and Veterans of Foreign Wars of America.

The inscription reads: "In memory of Elsie [sic] Winters Mitchell. The only adult civilian killed by an enemy instrument of war in the continental United States during World War II. Killed by a Japanese bomb in Bly, Oregon, May 6, 1945."

Elsye shares this piece of Port Angeles real estate, a large bluff overlooking the Strait of Juan de Fuca, with hundreds of other more anonymous and more famous people. Just a few feet away is a much bigger slab of black granite that marks the grave of one of Port Angeles's most famous residents, writer Raymond Carver, who has become a cult figure in Japan. On Memorial Day, the well-known and the obscure also share this space with the hundreds of tiny American flags distributed by the Daughters of the American Revolution.

Just to the right of the cemetery, around a bluff, sits the giant Daishowa America paper mill that employs more than three hundred Port Angeles residents. Aside from what she reads in the newspaper or hears from friends, Thelma doesn't know much about the new Japanese company. Since Archie developed a problem with his lungs and was put on an oxygen machine, it has been tough for the couple to get out of their house. But she talks to people at church and at least once a week goes out to practice with her singing group.

When Thelma first heard about Daishowa buying up the old "Crown Z mill," as she still calls it, she felt a little uneasy. Over the past few years, she has heard more and more about the Japanese buying up pieces of America, from New York skyscrapers to movie studios in Hollywood. She has no concrete evidence of wrongdoing, but she wonders whether there is more to the Japanese buying spree in America than she reads in her newspapers or hears on the evening news. She knows enough to be suspicious, but not enough to understand.

"I'm not sure I can really trust them," she said, referring to the Japanese investors in America.

Thelma has never met any of the Japanese managers who work at Daishowa's Port Angeles mill. But they know of her, or at least of her sister. Shortly after Daishowa took over the mill, a rumor began circulating around the mill that Daishowa was involved in building the balloon bombs. Down at the

Clallam County Veterans Center, the story was passed on by a Daishowa America employee, one of the older American guys who still remembers the war enough to cringe a little when he thinks about where his paycheck comes from.

David Schulz, one of Port Angeles's leading veterans' advocates, is convinced it is true. He doesn't have any evidence, other than the word of another World War II veteran. But for him, that's enough. "He oughta know," Schulz said, casting his allegiance with the guy who was on his side during the war. "I believe it."

Daishowa officials deny the company had any connection to the World War II balloon-bomb campaign, pointing out that the paper used to make the balloons was a handmade variety. But when the Fu-Go project moved into high gear, some of the paper and balloon panels were produced in factories. Mitsubishi Seishi, the Nippon Kakokin Co., and the Kokuka Rubber Co. were the firms a prominent historian cited in connection with the project.

Daishowa's official company history makes no mention of the balloon project, although several of its manufacturing plants were used to produce aircraft and engine parts. However, Japanese officials have stated that the balloon-bomb campaign was a top-secret operation, and individuals or companies were sometimes not told of their involvement. So on a theoretical level, it is possible that people connected with Daishowa could have contributed to the balloon-bomb campaign, just as many Americans participated in building weapons used to fight the Germans and Japanese.

On the personal level, however, fact and fiction often blur. In the 1970s, Teruo Kondo, a young Daishowa employee, was working in the company's Portland wood-purchasing office and enjoying the slow pace of life and easy access to outdoor recreation. His weekends were spent exploring the mountains or going out to the ocean beaches that were less than an hour's drive away.

Kondo developed a fondness for American beer, a devotion that brought him into direct conflict one night with a couple of drunks in a Portland bar. They called him a "Jap" and a "yellow monkey." He would have responded with his fists if a friend hadn't stepped in and stopped him.

Kondo is convinced that the tension in that bar had nothing to do with economic conflict or World War II in general. It was something much more personal. "During the war, Japan released some balloon bombs and they landed somewhere around Coos Bay, Oregon," Kondo said, when the incident came up in conversation years later. "I think these guys were relatives or friends of the victims. I think they were just angry."

In his mind, it was guilt by association, fifty years after the fact. Kondo was Japanese. It was the Japanese who launched those bombs. For some, the legacy of accusation and recrimination and guilt refuses to end, ricocheting back and forth across the Pacific Ocean on a jetstream of deep-felt emotion.

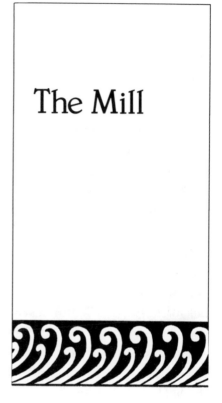

The Mill

I.

DAVE HOGLUND WAS WORKING the graveyard shift down at the paper mill on February 16, 1988; he had been warned to expect some lights and cameras when Daishowa America officially took control. He scanned the small crowd of Japanese businessmen—which included the new mill manager Yutaka Mochizuki—and they stared back with a look of expectation. It felt like one of those *Twilight Zone* episodes where a man goes to sleep and wakes up and finds out he is in the same place but at a different time. Things were the same but different.

Jokes are the standard tool for defusing tension around the paper machine, and Hoglund's boss kept kidding him about "dropping it down the hole." It would be tough to do, to drop the roll in the wrong way, since his entire body was trained to do things right. But anything was possible, especially on a day when everything seemed so out of kilter. "I'm gonna do it on purpose," Hoglund told his supervisor. "Just watch me."

They laughed. It was their way of reminding each other that nothing important had changed. The Japanese may have bought the real estate and the paper machines. But they hadn't bought Hoglund. Minutes ticked by. Shortly after eight A.M., the forty-seven-year-old papermaker dropped Daishowa America's first roll of American telephone-directory paper into place. As soon as that roll made its way through the machine, the lights and cameras disappeared. It was, by the standards of the moment, a success. There were no smear holes, no breaks. The roll of paper sped through the system and came off the other end.

Outside the main office, near the stone memorial to the two mill employees killed in World War II, Mochizuki and some other Daishowa officials gathered for a photo to commemorate the takeover. A brisk wind was blowing off the strait, and it was difficult to stand upright. A few quick photos were snapped, and the group dispersed to their offices. The lavish reception with the imported sushi chef and a speech by the governor, the visits by the Saito family—that would all come later. Daishowa's officials deliberately chose not to have a big ceremony to mark the transfer of power for fear they would further alarm the employees, more than a dozen of whom were already making plans for early retirement.

In the photographic records of that moment, Hoglund and Mochizuki are members of Daishowa's extended family, smiling accessories to a significant moment in the company history. But photos, in their ability to freeze time, can be remarkably accurate or incredibly misleading. What photos have difficulty recording is the ambivalence of human feelings, the ability to accept and reject, admire and fear, love and hate, all at the same time.

For Hoglund, the Japanese were the stuff of World War II movies and business-news headlines. He didn't know any Japanese people and certainly hadn't spent a lot of his waking moments worrying about what they were like. Until now, it had never occurred to him that his future might depend on one. Raised during a period when American values and the English language reigned supreme, he found himself in a world where his paycheck was controlled by people and laws formed beyond his linguistic reach. While his parents and grandparents faced the Great Depression, wars, and the invention of the television, he confronted the equally frightening prospect of a technological revolution in which the people he understood—even if he didn't like them—were no longer calling the shots.

The danger zones in this global society, the places where a person could walk right off the edge of common sense without knowing it, were much tougher to find and navigate. Crossing a cultural divide without a map is perilous. And in the inevitable way that miscommunication breeds miscommunication, this tale of Port Angeles in the 1990s was one where small events threatened to become international incidents and innocent people got caught in the middle.

One hundred and sixty years after the shipwrecked sailors from Japan washed up on a western Washington beach, the employees of an American paper mill were being pushed into the Pacific Century by forces as mystifying as a powerful jetstream of air or current of water. For Hoglund, a man who had never had any desire to venture beyond Canada, the land of sushi and on-time delivery was as exotic as the whale-hunting Native Americans were to those first three Japanese visitors.

But like the sailors, whose only hope of survival was the very people portrayed by their government as the enemy, Hoglund was being forced to look for his future across the Pacific. And he wasn't sure that he liked what he saw for himself or his children.

•   •   •

THERE HAVE BEEN MILLS in Hoglund's life as far back as he can remember. His father, Lloyd Hoglund, a second-generation millworker from Minnesota, was a saw filer, a throwback to the generation when millworkers were master craftsmen and products were produced by people with the help of machines, rather than the other way around. In the hierarchy of the mill, a saw filer was a specialist, expected to be able to take a four- or five-pound hammer and pound a sharpened circle saw into shape.

It was the elder Hoglund's quest for a head saw filer's job that kept his family moving across Washington State, from mill to mill, town to town. The senior Hoglund hunted and fished and kept the freezer filled with venison and salmon. His sons learned early in life that they needed to look after their own needs, which included working two paper routes for spending money.

Any child that grows up in a mill family knows the downside, especially the shift work: fathers who disappeared in the evenings or weekends and slept through the day, leaving a legacy of missed football games, piano recitals, and Christmas concerts; fathers so stressed out from the latest emergency—a broken paper machine, a cracked waste pipe—that the bar was the first place they headed after closing time.

Hoglund attended elementary school in Aberdeen, a mill town southwest of Port Angeles on the Washington coast, where he got his first taste of union politics. No one said anything about a strike, but one day, his dad stopped going to work and the refrigerator started getting emptier and emptier. The elder Hoglund, a small wiry man who spoke when he was spoken to, told Dave to climb into the family's old pickup truck, and they drove out to an ocean beach that has since been claimed by expensive hotels and condominiums. After digging a couple of buckets of clams, they drove a little farther down the road and stopped to cut a load of firewood. When the refrigerator and woodpile were empty, they went back again. Hoglund's father never offered any lectures on the importance of unions—that wasn't his style. But by the end of that summer, when his father had returned to work, the taste of clams and union politics were all mixed up in his young son's mind.

By the time the elder Hoglund landed a job at the Merrill

& Ring sawmill in Port Angeles in 1957, his son was getting ready to graduate from high school. Dave's ambitions were modest: a good-paying job in a quiet place where the animals outnumbered the people; a home; and, eventually, a family.

The northern coast of the Olympic Peninsula was an out-doorsman's dream: forests filled with towering Douglas firs; trails leading to mountain peaks scaled only by those willing to work hard for their solitude; fishing holes and mountain lakes that promised freezers full of plump trout, steelhead, and salmon; hunting grounds that still produced enough deer to provide an occasional trophy for marksmen unfazed by rain or bone-chilling winds.

In those days, Port Angeles was, in the best sense of the word, a mill town. With five big paper and lumber mills—and a number of smaller operations—it was tough to find someone who did not have a relative or friend working at a mill. Then, as now, the mills were known for providing good-paying, steady work. Not the flashiest work, and certainly not as adventurous or dangerous as the jobs in the woods. In a timber economy that judged its men by their brawn, the mill jobs ranked low on the macho scale but high on reliability. Few kids said between swigs of beer, "Boy, I'd really like to get a job at the mill when I graduate." But for someone who preferred to watch the world from the sidelines, it was the right place to enter adulthood.

At that time, it wasn't uncommon to find two or three generations working side by side in a mill, since jobs were handed down like heirlooms. The Hoglunds were no excep-tion. One night, his father came home from the mill and told Dave to put on his boots. Later that evening, the third generation of Hoglunds began shoveling sawdust.

Two months later, in the inevitable ebb and flow of the Northwest wood products industry, Dave Hoglund was laid off. He ended up getting a job next door at the mill owned by Crown Zellerbach Corp., a San Francisco–based wood products company. At $2.05 an hour, the new job paid eight cents an hour more and also offered a day shift. Hoglund was, by mill standards, climbing the ladder.

When Hoglund joined the papermaking business, it required as much brawn as brain. Wood chips were fed into huge stone grinders that mashed them into pulp. The pulp was cleaned and mixed with chemicals that altered the consistency and color before being sent through the presses where it was flattened and the liquid was squeezed out. Every step of the process required human intervention: shoveling wood chips, gauging the right consistency and color, loading and unloading the rolls, adjusting the presses and the dryer. It was hot, dangerous work with plenty of room for error.

If a guy was lucky, and Hoglund was, he got on the good side of some old-timers who knew the ropes and were willing to pass on their knowledge. It was from them that he learned how to read a smear hole (the imperfections in the paper roll), which supervisors to avoid, and the best places to fish for steelhead. It was also from them that he learned about the growing dissatisfaction with the two unions that represented more than twenty-one thousand workers in forty-nine paper mills around the United States: the International Brotherhood of Pulp, Sulphite, and Paper Mill Workers; and the United Papermakers and Paperworkers.

Two years into his career at the mill, Hoglund discovered why the older guys were so angry. He walked into the laboratory, where he had gotten a job as a technician, and pulled out his time card to clock in. There, much to his surprise, he saw he had been given a raise—of sorts. He didn't even know the union had been negotiating a new contract. And now, some nameless guy on the East Coast had signed away another couple of years of his life for a nickel an hour more. No longer a rookie, he wanted a living wage.

But it wasn't until 1964, sparked by a dispute over the selection of a key union leader, that a group of West Coast union leaders mounted a rebellion and successfully formed the Association of Western Pulp and Paper Workers (AWPPW). The breakaway union was immediately thrust into contract negotiations; within days the talks broke down.

Hoglund and his nineteen-year-old-wife, Marcy, barely a year into their marriage, had just put a thousand dollars down on a three-bedroom house on two acres of land, leaving them with fifty dollars in the bank. Marcy, who was seven months pregnant with their first child, packed for the move while her husband took off on his annual hunting trip. Part way through the trip, one of the men had to leave early to go back to work at the mill. He told his friends he would be back to hunt if the union ended up shutting down the mill. That evening, they looked up and saw him walking toward them.

Luckily for them, the strike was, as strikes go, relatively short. But for Hoglund, it was a brutal introduction to life on the wrong side of the law. When the picketers tried to stop the trucks from entering the mill property, the police stepped in with teargas and threats of jail. Tempers flared when a couple of union members, both relief supervisors, crossed the picket line. In the union bible, that was turning on a family when it was down, the kind of betrayal for which there is no forgiveness. After ten days of bitterness, a contract was signed and the millworkers returned to their jobs. But Hoglund watched as some of his more militant colleagues got their revenge on one man who had sold his loyalty to the company. The verbal taunts and ugly graffiti on the wall finally drove "the traitor" away.

Through the decade of the Beatles and the Vietnam War, the Hoglunds raised two kids, Steven and Rebecca, traded in their cottage for a family-sized house and went on strike with some regularity. The AWPPW contracts ran from one to three years, and every negotiation featured several months of angry rhetoric exchanged between the company and the union before the threat of a strike arose. Every second or third negotiation, the talks would break down and the pickets would go up. It usually happened in the fall. Hoglund and his friends would go salmon fishing or hunting when they weren't on the picket line.

The reward for the weeks without pay, the long hours on the picket line, the stomach-wrenching ugliness, was a couple of decades worth of pay raises and extra benefits that pushed the millworkers to the top of the industrial heap. But the glory days of the union were drawing to a close in America. National union leaders settled into comfortable, often high-paying jobs, and began losing touch with the union members. Mechanization and competition from low-wage countries contributed to a shrinkage in heavily unionized manufacturing industries while the new jobs were gained in areas without ties to blue-collar America or unions. And rumors of mob connections and financial scandals touched the highest echelons of America's most powerful unions.

Port Angeles was changing too, attracting disillusioned baby boomers in search of clean air and safe streets, and retirees looking for an inexpensive place to enjoy golf and bridge. Foreign competitors and high interest rates—whch depressed the national housing market—took their toll on the Northwest wood-products industry. One after another, the smaller sawmills closed down.

In 1978, Crown Zellerbach issued an ultimatum to the AWPPW after negotiations failed: Back to work or be replaced. The union members stayed on the picket line; and the company shipped in managers from all over the United States to cross those lines and start up the paper machines on Ediz Hook. As weeks dragged into months, there was talk of homes being repossessed, nervous breakdowns, and plots to seek revenge by shutting down the mill with explosives.

Hoglund didn't hold a grudge against supervisors who came to work at the mill. But he still bristles when he recalls the townspeople who turned their backs on the picket signs, the restaurateurs who crossed the picket lines to feed the employees inside, and the truck drivers who drove past the picketers with loads of chips.

When the two sides finally made peace seven months later, the bitterness between union members and management turned daily contact into a form of guerrilla warfare. Like other U.S. pulp and paper manufacturers, the San Francisco company was under pressure from the government to invest money in its mills to meet stricter air- and water-quality regulations. Over the next decade, morale in Port Angeles worsened as Crown Zellerbach concentrated its money and attention on a five-hundred-million-dollar modernization of its huge mill in Camas, Washington. In private conversations, in company literature, and even in the mainstream media, the Port Angeles mill was labeled a cash cow to be milked for the rest of the company. For the millworkers, it was a humiliating reminder that they were the B-team.

Deep in debt, but rich in timberland, the San Francisco corporation caught the eye of a British financier with a nasty reputation for buying up troubled companies and tearing them apart for a profit. After months of jockeying, Sir James Goldsmith won control of the company in 1985 and forced it to split up its holdings and sell them off piecemeal. James River Corp. purchased all the Crown Zellerbach mills, including the one in Port Angeles.

Within three weeks, James River began pumping money into the Port Angeles mill. Over the next year $4.7 million was spent to modernize two paper machines. Millworkers celebrated by buying new houses and fishing boats. They were working for a company with financial resources and a good reputation—and it was still an American company.

But as the weeks turned into months, Hoglund began to get a vague feeling of uneasiness. James River hadn't even put up a new sign to commemorate its takeover. There was no embossed stationery, no flag-waving, chest thumping, none of the traditional signs of pride that accompany a transfer of corporate ownership.

Something wasn't right.

•   •   •

IN 1945, KANEZO AND TOMEKO MOCHIZUKI OF NAGOYA, Japan, had their first child, Yutaka. It was not the most auspicious time for him to be born—brought into a country that had spent all its natural and unnatural resources on the losing end of the world's second great war. Nagoya was not a target of the two atomic bombs dropped by the United States on Japan, but it was one of many cities decimated by air raids and firebombs.

When Tomeko was pregnant with Yutaka, the first of three children, the family house was set ablaze during a bombing raid. She narrowly escaped with a few clothes and diapers, items too precious to leave to the flames. Kanezo, who served in the Japanese Imperial Navy, was badly injured in a battle at sea. He returned home with just one lung, his crippled respiratory system a constant reminder of how close he had come to being one of the nation's war dead.

In Nagoya, as in other big cities, the survivors scrambled to rebuild a life out of the rubble after Japan's surrender. There were estimates that as many as one third of Japan's urban areas were destroyed and more than eight million people left homeless. Food coupons were useless because the stores had been emptied by black marketeers who sold the goods for more than a hundred times their value. Housewives traveled to the countryside to trade in their silk kimonos and silver heirlooms for rice or vegetables. During that first cold winter, many went without fuel and warm clothing. Thousands died of starvation and exposure.

When there was no rice at the Mochizuki dinner table, the ceramic bowls were filled with potatoes or squash. Yutaka, who goes by the name Tad, still remembers, in vivid detail, the year he got a banana for his birthday.

There are many who believe those difficult postwar years fostered the Japanese people's fear of dependency and their drive to achieve. But it is difficult to measure accurately the impact of a trauma on the psyche of a nation. At one level, the Japanese debate over self-sufficiency in rice production is clearly self-serving politics and protectionism. On a more personal level, it is informed by the memory of a hungry child watching his parents trade away their most precious belongings for a bag of rice or a couple of scrawny chickens.

The war was, in one sense, a great leveler. While his father worked his way up the ladder at Nissan, Tad was working his way through a Japanese education system stripped of references to the national symbols banned by General Douglas MacArthur, the leader of the occupation forces. The Rising Sun did not fly on flagpoles. There was no national anthem sung at school assemblies. Rather than building paper balloons, the emperor's children were asked to resurrect the nation's integrity through hard work and cooperation.

By the time he entered the University of Hokkaido in the mid-1960s, the "Made in Japan" label was turning up on cheap toys and electronic goods all over the world. As the eldest son, Tad Mochizuki had an obligation to take care of his mother and father; he decided to eschew a career in high technology or finance for the more humble world of milk because there was a big dairy producer in Nagoya.

The Japanese economy didn't cooperate with his plans. By the time Mochizuki graduated in 1969 with a degree in agriculture, there were no jobs in the dairy industry. His second choice was the pulp-and-paper industry. While Oji Paper, the country's largest and most prestigious paper company, wasn't hiring, there was, however, Daishowa Paper Mfg. Co., which had plans to build a mill in Nagoya. He took the two-day examination with 250 other applicants. Two days later, he got a call at his parents' home in Nagoya. That summer, he became one of seventy new members of the Daishowa family.

For an ambitious young man, Mochizuki couldn't have made a better choice. In 1939, Chiichiro Saito, an entrepreneurial tea farmer from Fuji City, at the base of Mount Fuji, had merged five small paper companies into Daishowa Paper Mfg. Co. Like most Japanese companies, Daishowa emerged from World War II with just a quarter of its manufacturing capacity in use. But the upstart paper manufacturer was a beneficiary of MacArthur's plan to rid Japan of the powerful *zaibatsu*, the corporate families that dominated the Japanese economy prior to the war. One of the largest *zaibatsu* was the Mitsui Group, whose members included Oji, Jujo, and Honshu Papers, the nation's three largest paper companies. When the Japanese government dissolved the Mitsui Group, and disrupted the traditional business relationships, the door cracked open wider for a newcomer willing to hustle. Paper consumption is a reliable barometer of economic health; the higher the growth rate, the more copy paper, toilet paper, and wrapping paper a society uses. In the 1950s and 1960s—as Japan's gross national product steadily climbed—Daishowa grabbed an increasing share of the society's expanding paper needs.

Daishowa's biggest hurdle was a lack of trees, since most of Japan's harvestable timberland was already contracted out to Oji, Honshu, or Jujo Paper. That forced the Saito family to concentrate on developing new ways of recycling waste paper. After Chiichiro's death in 1961, his eldest son, Ryoei, took control of the company and began exploring other sources of raw materials. At the urging of a friend, Saito traveled to the Pacific Northwest to look at the mountains of wood chips being created by the prolific Northwest timber companies. In the early 1960s, he became the first Japanese company to import wood chips from the United States to make pulp.

In an industry renowned for its stodginess, Saito was a rebel, borrowing heavily from the banks to expand his paper empire throughout Japan, Australia, Malaysia, and Canada. He liked to experiment, putting his researchers to work developing paper out of pulp from eucalyptus and rubber trees, the latter a commercial failure. His timber-buying operations in the ecologically sensitive regions of Australia and Canada prompted protests from environmentalists. He also invested heavily in golf courses, hotels, and an art collection that included Picassos, Klees, and Chagalls. By 1981, Daishowa's debts were twice its annual sales.

In an unusually public confrontation, Sumitomo Bank, the company's largest shareholder, took control of Daishowa in 1982 and removed Saito and his sons from the management team. Kikuzo, Ryoei's younger brother, was installed as president. The company's debts were reduced by half, and assets—including Saito's European masterpieces—were sold.

When the elder Saito regained control of the company a year later, he promptly cut all ties with Sumitomo and eventually removed his brother from the presidency. And contrary to the maxim of live and learn, he simply stepped back into his job and did more of the same, as if to show the bank and his critics that he simply didn't care.

One of the first things on his list was getting into the North American market, an expensive and risky proposition at a time when the world was oversupplied with paper, and the environmental movement was starting to gain public credibility in its campaign to preserve the world's dwindling stands of old-growth forests.

In September 1985, the finance ministers of the top five industrial nations met in the Plaza Hotel in New York and forged an agreement to push the U.S. dollar lower, an act of fiscal wizardry designed to make U.S. products more competitive overseas and reduce the trade deficit. The Plaza Accord, as the agreement came to be known, resulted in a dramatic depreciation of the dollar and doubled the buying power of the Japanese yen. By early 1988, the yen had appreciated from 240 to 120 to the dollar.

Armed with cheap capital, Japanese investors dramatically expanded their worldwide buying spree. In 1988, Japanese companies invested $15.1 billion in U.S. companies, real estate, and other assets, compared with $6.2 billion the previous year. Fiscally starved state governments dispatched delegations to Japan armed with valuable incentives: tax breaks, job-training subsidies, paved roads, and low-priced utilities.

Japan still ranked number three in direct investment in the United States, behind Britain and the Netherlands. But the dramatic rise in Japanese investment alarmed many, including Representative John Bryant, an outspoken Texas Democrat, who warned that the United States was endangering its future by "selling off the family jewels" to foreigners. In Honolulu, the spread of Japanese investment prompted town meetings and calls for a ban on foreign investment.

For a man who loathes negative publicity, Saito couldn't have chosen a worse time to invest in America. But he was convinced that Japan's position in the world economy would be forever limited by its lack of natural resources, and that the best base for an international paper company was North America, the center of the world's largest market and an easy stepping-stone to Europe or the rest of Asia.

After several other deals fell through, Steve Taniguchi, who headed up Daishowa America Co. Ltd., the company's U.S. subsidiary, persuaded Saito to look at the James River mill in Port Angeles. James River, a producer of high-end specialty papers, didn't have a place in its operation for an aging mill that produced cheap paper for telephone directories.

Port Angeles offered Saito a deepwater port, an abundant source of clean water, a stable wood supply, a hardworking population, and politicians hungry for new sources of jobs and tax dollars. Even more significant, from the business standpoint, were two dams on the Elwha River that provided 40 percent of the mill's electrical power at a very low cost.

Daishowa courted James River for two years. The negotiations were complicated by a host of issues, including the transfer of a labor agreement with the Association of Western Pulp and Paper Workers, one of the region's most militant unions, and a complex legal entanglement over the federal licensing of the two aging dams, the Elwha and the Glines. In the end, James River, which owned the dams, agreed to keep them until the licensing process was completed.

By the time the final papers were signed in February 1988, Saito was convinced he needed a mill manager who wouldn't be intimidated by ancient paper machines, a strong union, and a work force that viewed change as just another step backward. Around the hallways of Daishowa headquarters, employees joked that working for Daishowa was like working for the Mafia: When Godfather Saito snapped his fingers, you jumped to attention. But when the call came to move to America, Tad Mochizuki didn't want to go.

•   •   •

IT WAS NOT a matter of ambition. If Mochizuki stayed in Japan, he might have labored away for another decade or two before gaining the kind of power and freedom he would enjoy as the first man to head up Daishowa's American mill. At the age of forty-three, he would be in charge of everything: budget, personnel, and machinery.

Since joining Daishowa, Mochizuki had earned a reputation as a problem solver. Shortly after he started working for the company, the Hokkaido mill had to be shut down for repairs. The enthusiastic young recruit didn't go home to sleep until the paper machine was up and running three days later. Working long days and weekends was part of his routine.

Mochizuki was a scientist by training and a perfectionist by personality, someone who saw a world of calculable probability providing little room for error. Like most Type-A personalities, he held the rest of the world to high standards but saved his roughest criticisms for himself. His knowledge of the way things worked—the how-to side of things—earned him the respect, but not always the friendship, of many.

Every five or six years, he was promoted to a job with more responsibility and given a more prestigious job title. After eleven years at the company's mill in Hokkaido, where he oversaw a major paper-machine rebuild, he was moved to the company's main mill in Fuji City and promoted to paper-machine superintendent. It was there that he caught the attention of Daishowa's head office in Tokyo.

Mochizuki's lack of enthusiasm for the Port Angeles assignment was not related to his abilities. It was a fear of things American: a language he couldn't speak; a people he didn't understand; and a country that seemed to radiate dislike at every opportunity. Foreigners, particularly Americans, didn't seem to like or trust the Japanese. At least that was the message broadcast loud and clear in the Japanese media, in articles about Japan-bashing politicians, and in the endless replays of the U.S. politicians smashing a Toshiba radio on the Capitol steps.

Mochizuki looked across the Pacific and saw that the American discomfort with, and resentment of, Japan's growing impact on the U.S. economy was being extended to its corporate representatives. A whole new list of stereotypes was attached to the Japanese: lavish spenders, arrogant, reclusive, clubbish, not generous enough in the community. His best friend, another Daishowa manager who worked in Canada, had been attacked by egg-throwing environmentalists angered by the company's decision to log a piece of Canadian timberland valued for its pristine wilderness.

At home, the news of his impending transfer was the focus of some unhappy discussions. His wife, Fumiko, a petite, outgoing woman he met in a college archery class, had no interest in living in America. Back in high school, she and her friends used to love going to American movies, particularly anything featuring Audrey Hepburn or lavish musicals like *The Sound of Music* and *South Pacific*. But when her best friend took additional English classes and signed up for a high-school exchange program in the United States, there was no persuading Fumiko to join her.

Over the years, Fumiko's vision of America continued to be shaped by Hollywood movies, television news, and newspaper reports. Lovesick couples and tap-dancing comics gave way to drugrunners and crime families with Italian names and hot tempers. Annette Funicello and Clark Gable were replaced by Charles Bronson and Sylvester Stallone. The postwar picture of *Leave It to Beaver* started to fray at the edges, unable to compete with the much flashier images of J. R. Ewing and his clan of scheming relatives.

To a woman raised in postwar Japan, America was a bewildering montage of stories about sinking test scores, guns in schools, racial tension in urban neighborhoods, and a growing resentment of its wealthier Asian neighbors. "What if their neighbors hated them?" she thought. "How would the children do in school?"

The Mochizuki children were her biggest headache. Makoto, a junior high school student, thought it might be fun to go to the land of Tom Cruise and pro football. But his elder brother, Akira, a junior in high school, was already starting to prepare for the highly competitive college exams that determine who makes the grade in Japanese society. Those accepted into Japan's best colleges—with Tokyo University at the top of the heap—are the ones offered jobs with the nation's top companies. Stepping off the educational track would put Akira at a disadvantage in competing for those coveted university slots. Even his teacher recommended against moving him. But the Mochizukis had no one in Fuji City who could take on a high-school boy for two years. Their nearest relatives lived hundreds of miles away. And they certainly weren't going to leave Akira alone.

Reminiscent of the shipwrecked Japanese of the nineteenth century, today's modern Japanese pioneers are forging a new image for a country whose growing economic clout has turned it into a threat around the world. Like their predecessors, they run the danger of being viewed upon their return as contaminated, or changed, by their foreign exposure. Instead of the threat of death, they face ostracism and suspicion from a society that shows little compassion for those who step outside society's rigid constraints.

The American values of independence, bluntness, and honesty—however real or imagined—are at odds with the Japanese emphasis on cooperation, face-saving, and teamwork. Given that difference, an overseas posting, considered by most Americans as a prestigious step up the career ladder, offers many personal and professional risks to a Japanese.

Early in Japan's overseas expansion, it was common for men to leave their families behind so the children would not be penalized for breaking out of the traditional mold. But Mochizuki wasn't willing to pay that high a personal price. Fumiko, on the other hand, was not willing to compromise her children's best interests just to meet society's demands. She already knew what it was like to buck convention, having chosen to continue pursuing a career in child development even after her two sons were born. After weeks of indecision, she finally told Tad to go ahead by himself. She would stay home with the boys against the wishes of her husband and her in-laws.

Mochizuki was a reluctant recruit, drafted to lead a group

of hostile strangers on foreign turf, using a language he could barely speak or understand. But in a land where personal integrity is directly tied to the fulfillment of obligation to family, company, and country, he never really had a choice. He was a Daishowa man.

•   •   •

PAPERMAKING IS STILL A HOT, messy business, but much of what used to be done with brawn and intuition is now handled by high technology. Characteristics critical to the final product—speed, wetness, heaviness, thickness—are monitored continually by banks of computers. Imperfections that used to be checked visually—color, holes, or wet spots—are found and marked by machine. Computers follow the stock from the headbox, which monitors consistency, to the fourdrinier wire, a moving screen that drains the water from the thin sheet of pulp and eventually feeds the paper into a maze of presses and dryers.

The papermaking industry has become such a technologically sophisticated business that the incremental steps required to stay ahead of the competition are million-dollar risks. One paper machine is a $150-million investment, a thoroughbred race horse of the industrial age. Daishowa's Port Angeles mill, which had two machines, was a small operation.

During his first few months in Port Angeles, Mochizuki was often found in his office reading papers well past midnight: financial records, production schedules, personnel reports. One thing was clear from the beginning: the lack of investment in the mill's infrastructure—everything from the production facilities to the equipment—had cut deeply into morale, production efficiency, and paper quality.

Within weeks of Daishowa's takeover, money started to flow into the company. The Daishowa America sign went up the day after the takeover. Hundreds of thousands of dollars were spent on painting and cleaning up the mill from the inside out. Old rusting machinery was hauled away. Leaking roofs were repaired. Even the employee shower room got a fresh coat of paint. Five million dollars was spent to upgrade the pulp-screening process and improve the computerized monitoring system.

When equipment needed to be replaced, Mochizuki usually chose the top-of-the-line brands—names like Beloit and Black Clawson. Competitors would look at the money flowing into that old mill on Ediz Hook and shake their heads in jealousy or amazement. "I think they wasted a lot of money," said one official of ITT Rayonier, after touring the plant.

But Mochizuki wasn't just buying incremental improvements in speed or quality, although those would show up in the short run. Top-quality equipment bought him flexibility, and that was what he wanted ten years down the line, when a computer in every home would reduce the need for telephone books. He needed to be able to switch his mill over to a line of paper with a future, perhaps the slick communication papers used in facsimile machines.

Mochizuki knew a smart mill manager could turn a profit with older machinery and undervalued employees for months, maybe even years. But eventually, morale would plunge, the machinery would begin breaking down more frequently, and the quality of the paper would suffer. It was a scene repeated over and over during the 1970s and 1980s, when the average rate of capital invested by American companies slipped behind that of their top foreign competitors.

Out on the floor of the paper mill, the Daishowa way of doing business was felt almost immediately. The learning curve was steep and brutal. The old adage at the mill—"If it's white, sell it"—wasn't good enough anymore. What used to go out to the customer—a roll of paper with a couple of small smear holes or a slightly off-color shade of yellow—was sent back to be turned into pulp. Every pulped roll of paper was a four-thousand-dollar loss, and the rolls of rejects, a mountain of failure, piled up those first few months.

There was a constant challenge to improve. Every day, the supervisors got a report on how their paper, and their competition's product, was performing in the customers' pressrooms. That information was passed on to the mill employees. Day after day, Hoglund's crew was told how well the paper produced by their Canadian competitor, MacMillan Bloedel, was performing on the printing presses.

Mochizuki inched the mill standards up, forcing his employees to readjust their personal level of quality or pay the consequences. Doing it right the first time became a lot easier than figuring out what went wrong and starting over again. And under the Japanese, the margin of error kept shrinking. In the past, for example, if the wire former was making a tiny hole in the paper, the roll would still be sent on to the customer. But under Daishowa, the papermakers were expected to follow the string of tiny pinholes to the source. If they couldn't find the place where the problem started, they were expected to pull out earlier rolls until that very first pinhole appeared. Then, the entire batch would be rejected and sent back to be turned into pulp.

At least once a week, often on Saturdays, Mochizuki would

take a walk through the paper mill after his morning meeting. He would stop and watch the paper machines in operation, say hello, and ask a question or two. The deafening roar of the machines crashing along at more than a thousand feet per minute, and Mochizuki's superficial grasp of the English language, made it tough to carry on a conversation. For the most part, he was treated like a special guest, afforded polite acknowledgments and a superficial exchange of information. He would make a suggestion, maybe recommend a new type of oil for lubricating the machines, and watch the heads nod. Two weeks later, he would return and find they were still using the old stuff.

Operating under Mochizuki's critical gaze made Hoglund and his coworkers nervous, sometimes to the point where they made stupid mistakes. Under Crown Zellerbach or James River, it was rare for the mill's top manager to pay a visit to the floor. Among themselves, they referred to the Japanese managers as their "shadows" because they seemed to be second-guessing every move. In a way, they were right. As Mochizuki walked through the mill, he took mental notes on how his employees did their jobs: to whom they talked; how they reacted to problems; what they did when things were quiet. He had figured out their equipment and their product. Now, he needed to get to know them.

Mochizuki had been in the business long enough to know how the dance of the papermakers should work. What he saw, again and again, was a collection of individual performances. In most cases, they were working hard, and in many instances, they were doing a pretty good job. But rarely did he see them working with each other: sharing information, consulting on problems, or stepping in to do someone else's job if needed. It was as if they were all operating in their own little orbits, intersecting as little as possible. It was an environment in which cooperation equaled failure. In just a few months, the Japanese mill manager had succeeded in raising individual standards of quality. But at some point, top efficiency could only be reached through the type of teamwork that led to creative solutions and an elevation of overall morale.

Mochizuki had spent enough Saturdays on the floor to make some judgments about his work force. In any large company, anywhere in the world, there were some employees who didn't want to work, had drug or alcohol problems, or were too old or set in their ways to learn something new. They had them in Fuji City; they had them in Port Angeles.

But his problem wasn't sloth or stupidity. It was a wall of American individualism, an elevation of turf, territory, and ego above everything else, that he just couldn't figure out. Weeks passed, and his suggestions were still going nowhere. He was beginning to feel as if the war he was waging was not with his competitors, but with his own employees. And from the perspective of someone who wanted to change the status quo, that was undeniably true.

What Mochizuki regarded as individualism bordering on selfishness was also a central pillar of the American labor system. While the concept of collective bargaining assumes a group of individuals working toward a united goal, American union philosophy also elevates the rights of the individual above the corporation.

Japan's rapid expansion into the United States had collided with American unions already disenchanted with the loss of jobs in the American auto industry to foreign competitors. Examples of Japan's success in working with American workers were overshadowed by the horror stories of unions frozen out by companies established by Japanese firms. In the Midwest, union officials and black community leaders accused Japanese manufacturers of avoiding establishing plants in areas with a heavy union presence or a large minority community.

In the Pacific Northwest, a region that had imported cheap Asian labor for more than two centuries, the labor community did not always speak with one voice on the issue of foreign involvement in the domestic economy. In the late 1800s and early 1900s, Northwest labor leaders led the movement to stop the immigration of Chinese and Japanese workers and supported laws that prevented them from owning land and gaining citizenship. Most unions also denied membership to Asians, forcing them to form their own collective-bargaining groups.

In the 1980s, the growing economic strength of Japan and other Asian countries could not be ignored by Northwest labor unions. However, the protests against imports and the "Buy American" campaign led by national labor unions didn't attract as large a following in Washington state, where one out of five jobs was dependent on foreign trade. While many labor leaders privately voiced fears about the growing clout of a powerful economic force with a much different attitude toward workers' rights, there was no loud outcry for shutting down the borders.

To a work force under pressure to modernize, mechanize, and globalize, Daishowa was a benefactor and a threat. It saved the mill's employees from the welfare line and kept a $26-million annual payroll flowing through the Port Angeles economy. But the new Japanese owners also brought with them new faces, a foreign language, and a very different way of doing business.

To prepare the Port Angeles mill for the twenty-first century, Mochizuki needed a team of true believers. But he knew a group of Americans couldn't be forced to adopt an attitude of collegiality and cooperation, especially if it was regarded as "Japanese management." They had to discover on their own the meaning of teamwork and sacrifice and devotion to a cause. They would be his pilgrims. He would provide the Mecca.

II.

LATE IN THE SUMMER OF 1988, a notice went up on the bulletin board in the mill. Crown Zellerbach and James River occasionally sent employees to visit pressrooms or attend a papermaking seminar in another city. Hoglund and some of his friends had once driven to Camas, Washington, down by the Oregon border, to take a look at a new paper machine installed at the James River mill. But this offer seemed unbelievable: a free trip for four papermakers to the corporate homeland, Japan.

Hoglund didn't give it much thought. The note said the company was looking for machine tenders, the people in charge of the wet end of the papermaking process. He was a back winder on the dry end. Besides, he couldn't believe they would choose a guy who had turned down at least one offer of a supervisor's job because it involved too many headaches for too little money.

Days passed. No one signed up.

Mochizuki couldn't figure it out. The supervisors told him that their employees didn't want to be away from their families for a month. "A month," he thought to himself, remembering his decision to leave his family for four years. A month barely rated as an absence by Japanese standards. One supervisor suggested shortening the trip to two weeks or sending the families along. But this wasn't supposed to be a vacation. A compromise was reached at three weeks, and the sign-up sheet was expanded to include anyone working on the paper machines. The sheet still remained empty.

Matt Bryant, a machine tender on the number two paper machine, wanted to go. But he was president of Local 169 of the AWPPW, and some of the other union officials were convinced the company was trying to brainwash its work force and buy off its leaders. They said anyone who accepted the trip was a sellout. Bryant, a thirty-two-year-old dark-haired man with nearly a decade in union politics, was stubborn. He didn't like anyone, union or management, telling him what to do. He thought it was a great chance to find out more about Daishowa and see how they treated their employees in Japan, a sort of reconnaissance mission. He finally signed up, telling his wife it was a "once-in-a-lifetime" opportunity.

More days passed. Henry Smedley, the paper-machine superintendent, asked Hoglund if he had ever considered signing up for the trip. "No, not really," was the reply. "Well, think about it," his boss said.

Hoglund, who had never left the continental United States except to visit Canada, went home to discuss the offer with Marcy. In their three decades of marriage, they had never been separated for more than a week at a time. Marcy told her husband he should go, since he might never again have a chance to visit Japan on someone else's dollar.

Hoglund went back to work the next day and told Smedley he was interested. The final two recruits were Ed Adamich, fifty-two, a thirty-year mill veteran with a reputation for speaking his mind, and Leon Hallman, forty-five, a soft-spoken mill-owner's son who had joined the company right out of the navy.

As soon as the four names were known, the whispering began. Many of their coworkers were just curious. Where are you going? What are you going to be doing? Others were much more vicious, accusing them of selling out to the Japanese and trying to win points with the new management. The criticism was particularly irritating to Bryant, because his leadership position in the union made him such an easy target. Hoglund just tried to ignore the ugly stuff. Accusations of favoritism were common in the power skirmishes that took place inside and outside the union.

But before long, Hoglund was kind of curious himself. Aside from some advice on the weather and what kind of clothes to pack, the four papermakers were given no instructions from the company about what to expect or how to act. There were no courses on the skills of business-card exchange and green-tea drinking, no handouts on cultural dos and don'ts, no explanation of who they would see or where they would go. And as the departure day drew near, it became more and more clear that they probably would not be receiving any.

Ever since the Japanese arrived in Port Angeles, there had been no shortage of plans: one-year plans, five-year plans, safety plans, remodeling plans, open-house plans. In the management corridors, they joked about the Daishowa two-hundred-year plan. But now that the company was going to the expense of sending four papermakers to Japan, could there really be no plan? At best, it seemed disorganized; at worst, sinister.

The day before they left, the four were called into Mochizuki's office, a cramped space in a glorified trailer in the corner of the mill parking lot. It was Mochizuki's first meeting with the four and they were all nervous. The manager knew what he wanted to say, but he wasn't sure he could express his thoughts in English. In the end, he kept his speech short and to the point.

"The most important thing is safety," he recalled telling his employees. "Japanese safety procedures are a very different style. The second requirement is health. The change of water and change of food. You must keep healthy. And third, you must learn some papermaking."

Mochizuki was distracted at that meeting by other problems, most notably another hitch in the company's effort to move forward on its multimillion-dollar mill expansion. Unless the company moved quickly, Daishowa would lose its opportunity to get a jump on the competition by adding two high-quality paper machines. Environmentalists and leaders of the local crafts unions had blocked Daishowa's efforts to get the necessary permits for the expansion, raising concerns about the impact on traffic, housing availability, and air quality.

With a "good luck" and "farewell," Mochizuki sent the four papermakers back to the mill. He didn't waste time worrying about how these four men would handle their time in Japan. Even if they couldn't understand Japanese and hated sushi, they could still find a "Bigu Maku" hamburger. Hog-lund returned to his job more confused than ever. What did Mochizuki mean by "learn papermaking"? Between them they had nearly a century of papermaking experience; they could make paper as well as anyone. During a break, he pulled Smedley aside and told him he was worried that the Japanese wanted them to go over and become cheerleaders for the Dai-showa way of doing business. He warned his boss that he wasn't about to become a pawn for the new employers.

Back at home, Hallman was starting to get that nervous feeling in his stomach he always got when he left town, the feeling that his wife, Alyce, called "just not wanting to leave his family." It was nothing new. When they were newlyweds and back from their honeymoon, he got "sicker than a dog" when he had to turn around and return to the navy ship. The same thing happened when he left on his two-week hunting trips. But he was determined not to let it get in the way of this trip. He had fond memories of Japan from his navy days and was eager to return.

The other two workers didn't know anything about Hog-lund's worries and Hallman's stomach. They were wrapped up in their own problems, just trying to figure out what clothes to pack and making sure their families were taken care of during their absence.

Storm clouds were building, but no one bothered to look up.

•   •   •

MOCHIZUKI ALSO HAD SOME distractions at home. A few months after her husband left for the United States, Fumiko changed her mind about staying behind. One of her best friends, a professor at the University of Shizuoka, convinced her that America would be a fascinating place to study Western attitudes toward child development. She also didn't want her two sons to spend their adolescent years without their father.

Before Fumiko and the boys arrived in May 1988, Mochizuki had gone house hunting. He looked at dozens of homes in search of one that was conveniently located near the mill and the schools and not too ostentatious or flashy. He ended up buying a split-level house next to Peninsula College, the local community college, and across town from the other four Japanese managers. There would be no Japanese ghetto in Port Angeles. Contrary to earlier fears that Daishowa would import a boatload of employees, the company posted a very small contingent of Japanese managers to Port Angeles. In addition to Mochizuki, the first group of Japanese managers included Dave Tamaki, a former English teacher turned community liaison; Junko Kubota, the corporate comptroller; Tom Oshiro, who operated as the senior project engineer and long-term planner; and Nick Ishioka, a young, single engineer.

In Port Angeles, a new Asian face was always noticed. Until Daishowa arrived, the Japanese community in this isolated town was a handful of older women, mostly war brides, a few younger people who had followed their hearts or jobs to the peninsula, and a couple of Japanese businessmen who had come over to work in the wood-products industry. Several Chinese and Southeast Asian families also settled in the area.

The Mochizukis were introduced to Port Angeles by Evelyn Lydiard, an outgoing woman who had turned a child's fascination with Japan into a hobby that she carried throughout life. She made one of the first phone calls Mochizuki received after arriving in town, inviting the Japanese managers out for drinks and an evening at the Port Angeles Symphony. When she heard that Mochizuki's family was coming to join him, she volunteered her services.

Over time, Lydiard, the wife of Harry Lydiard, a veterinarian and former county commissioner, became the Mochizukis' interpreter of American life. Two days a week, she drove over to their home, took off her shoes at the door, and set herself up at the dining-room table surrounded by the family's collection of beautiful Japanese artwork and American kitsch. In the glass cases that lined the dining room, a display of dolls clothed in intricate silk kimonos shared a shelf with a collection of ceramic knickknacks common in seaside tourist shops.

From the living room, she could look out over Port Angeles harbor and even get a glimpse of the mill tucked off on one side. The living-room wall was decorated with a picture of Mount St. Helens, the Washington volcano that erupted in 1980, and a collection of fake license plates bearing the names of cities visited by the family during their stay in the United States.

Like a queen holding court, Lydiard would gather Fumiko, Akira, and Makoto around the dining-room table with their books and questions. For an hour, she would counsel and coach and answer questions as best she could. "What is the role of volunteer organizations?" Fumiko might ask. "What is an SAT test?" was a more likely question from the boys.

With the help of Lydiard and Terry Tamaki, Dave's wife, Fumiko set about creating a courseload in American life that kept her busy from dawn until dusk. Peninsula College offered a wide variety of classes for part-time students, and she was able to persuade the instructors to allow her to audit the courses until she could learn enough English to take the classes for grades. She visited schools and day-care centers to satisfy her curiosity about the American child-care system. In the evenings, she would curl up with her books and a Japanese-English dictionary.

An evening at Evelyn and Harry Lydiard's home—a Northwest ranch house tucked away on a wooded bluff above the Elwha River—was the Mochizukis' introduction to Port Angeles society. Their friends were on the board of the Port Angeles Fine Arts Center or the Port Angeles Symphony orchestra and had a predisposition for travel and a curiosity about the world. The Lydiards' friends became the Mochizukis' friends, sharing their interest in skiing and hiking, and providing advice on helping children navigate adolescence.

One issue that wasn't discussed at the Lydiards' dinner table was the future of the two dams on the Elwha River that provided low-cost energy to the Daishowa mill. Harry, an outdoorsman whose first love was his tree farm, believed fervently that the dams had destroyed a majestic river by cutting off its flow and throwing off the natural ecosystem. He supported a coalition of environmental groups, the Elwha Klallam tribe, and several federal agencies that had filed a lawsuit in federal court to prevent the relicensing of the dams. In the year since Daishowa had purchased the mill, the coalition had begun pushing for dam removal as the best option for restoring a free-flowing river that once supported fifty-pound chinook salmon.

The fate of the Elwha River was one of many areas where Evelyn and her strong-willed husband agreed to disagree. One

morning, she picked up the newspaper and saw her husband
quoted in an article on the dams. She quickly dashed off a
note to Tad Mochizuki, assuring him that she did not share
her husband's view and apologizing for her husband's public
opposition. Nothing more was said, and the subject of the
dams never again entered the relationship between the two
families.

The Mochizukis had far greater concerns at home, where
Akira, their eldest, was battling an acute case of homesickness.
Because of his limited knowledge of English, his parents had
decided to have him repeat his sophomore year at Port Angeles
Senior High School. As a result, he was way ahead of the other
students in math and science and couldn't understand more
than a couple of words of the lectures in history and English.
In the afternoons, he would come home from school, sleep for
several hours, eat dinner, and then study until past midnight.

As the days passed, Akira retreated further and further
behind a wall of unhappiness. Adolescence is rough enough
without the added burden of not being able to talk to your
peers. Akira wasn't particularly interested in sports and didn't
share his classmates' love of partying. Back home, his friends
were preparing for their college entrance exams, and he knew
that a knowledge of Northwest history wasn't going to be
worth much when he returned. Every month he was away
from Japan, the gulf between his desires and reality widened.

Makoto, who was enrolled in junior high, had no trouble
finding a shortcut to acceptance. He was a sports lover and
immediately hooked up with the boys who were stars of the
football and basketball teams. The sports-crazy, unscheduled
life of a junior-high jock fit his personality. He had no desire

to be back in Japan, where he would be attending a cram school in the evenings and on weekends to get ready for high school.

When Mochizuki looked at his two sons, with their diametrically opposed approaches to life in America, it was difficult not to feel guilty. Had he been wrong in bringing Akira here at such a critical time in his educational career, forcing him off a path that he might not have a chance to climb back on? And was his younger son in danger of becoming so American in his thinking that he would never be able to fit back into the rigid parameters of Japanese society? During those early months when homesickness occasionally reached crisis proportions, he wanted to remind his family that this was not to be forever. They would, at some point, return to Japan.

• • •

AS SOON AS HE WAS USHERED into a business-class seat on the plane to Japan, Hoglund knew that Daishowa intended to show him a good time. For just a moment, he felt a twinge of guilt. But he had a lot more important things to worry about. In order to prevent an embarrassing incident at a store counter or restaurant, he drew up a little crib sheet with some yen prices and their dollar equivalents. At the end of their first meal—at a sushi restaurant near the Marunouchi Hotel in Tokyo—he realized he hadn't gone high enough in his numbers. The tab for that meal—a bowl of rice, a dozen pieces of raw fish, and a couple of beers—added up to more than a hundred dollars. It was just the first of many jaw-dropping charges for meals on the Daishowa expense account.

By the time they woke up the next morning, Mochizuki's

three commandments—safety, health, and a willingness to learn—had already begun to unravel. Hallman emerged from his hotel room with more than jet lag. He felt sick—something to do with his stomach. Their worried hosts immediately took him to a doctor who spoke no English. Using one of the Daishowa employees as a translator, Hallman tried to explain how he felt: nausea and cramps, something that came and went without any explanation. The doctor gave him pills but couldn't explain in English what they were for. Listening to the rapid-fire exchanges in Japanese made Hallman's stomach hurt more.

Leaving the comfort zone of a primary language is a frustrating, and occasionally terrifying, experience. For Hallman, going to a doctor became a testament to faith when it became clear that he must simply take the translator's word that those pills wouldn't kill him and, in fact, might do him some good. For the others, the frustration registered in different forms: trying to make a phone call when the operator didn't speak English; or guessing which bottle on the drugstore shelf contained shampoo and which one cured indigestion.

Hoglund and the others suspected Hallman's stomach problems might be homesickness, something that pills couldn't cure. Around the Daishowa officials, Hallman played the good sport. But over the next few days, it was clear the pain was not going away. He told the others that he wanted to go home to a doctor whom he knew and could understand.

The Port Angeles papermakers were on a rigorous schedule that started at breakfast and lasted well into the evening. They were taken to Daishowa's Tokyo office, which overlooks the northern terminal of Tokyo Station, and exchanged small talk with the company's chairman, Ryoei Saito. Hoglund and the others walked away from that conversation thinking the Japanese billionaire was sort of a modest fellow, a "regular guy." They visited the mind-boggling display of consumer gadgets known as Akihabara, the electronics district, and got up at five A.M. to see gigantic frozen tuna auctioned off at the Tsukiji Fish Market. At night they were taken to hostess clubs in the Ginza, drank hundreds of dollars' worth of sake and whiskey, and even paid a visit to the famous Playboy Club. After a few days in Tokyo, they flew to the northern island of Hokkaido to tour Daishowa's Shiraoi mill, one of the company's largest pulp and paper operations. When their work was done, they were taken to a nearby hot springs resort where they sat in big rock pools of steaming water and danced late into the evening with attractive Japanese women wearing silk kimonos and pleasant smiles. Before leaving the island, they stopped at an Ainu village where descendants of Japan's original inhabitants demonstrated traditional dances and displayed trained bears. From there, they traveled to the northern tip of Honshu to visit the company's Iwanuma mill and returned to Tokyo on the bullet train.

This fast-track introduction to modern Japan became a whirl of new faces and polite smiles. They met dozens of Daishowa employees from mill managers to papermakers. They drank tea and coffee until they never again wanted to see another cup. Their stack of Japanese name cards outgrew their wallets.

This was certainly the Japan they had heard about, the land of punctuality and politeness and crime-free streets. But there were other things that no one had warned them about.

Like the sense of sameness. To their eyes, Japan looked like everyone came out of a similar mold. The dark-haired men on the streets in Tokyo wore dark suits, with an occasional red tie. The dark-haired men in the mills wore uniforms.

In a country where foreigners are still a rarity, the Port Angeles papermakers had plenty of reminders of their strangeness. Whether it was polite stares from fellow passengers on the bullet train, the giggles of young girls in school uniforms, or yet another encounter with a hotel bed that left their feet dangling over the edge, the message was clear: They didn't fit. One day, Bryant was sitting in the Marunouchi subway station in Tokyo, watching the ritual of mass transport, Japanese-style. The train pulled up to the platform, disgorged its passengers, and sucked up the next group of people. When he looked again, it was as if nothing had changed. There were the same dark-haired people reading the same newspapers. It reminded him of ants marching across the dirt to their subterranean home, orderly lines of similar faces crossing the station floor without colliding.

Hoglund, a small-town boy who complains when a half-dozen cars back up at a stoplight, marveled over the ability of millions of people to live with such civility in such a small place. He could walk outside his hotel at any hour of the day or night and not worry about getting mugged. Clean and polite, clean and polite. It was a circular tape, playing over and over again in his mind.

Adamich felt a different kind of culture shock. He was having a hard time reconciling the Japan he saw with the memories of his first visit as a young army soldier in the 1950s. Back then, when he was an eighteen-year-old kid preoccupied with having fun, Japan was a series of bars interspersed with hangovers. But he remembered enough to be shocked by what he saw on the bullet train from Tokyo to Fuji City, the home of Daishowa's main mill. Where he remembered old wooden structures and the ruins of burned-out homes, there were shiny high-rise buildings and boutiques carrying the latest designer fashions from Europe. Mile after mile of rice fields had shrunk to tiny postage stamps of green wedged between housing developments with blue-tiled roofs and giant neon signs. There wasn't much to separate one big city from the next. In the countryside, the small squares of green grew a bit larger and, occasionally, on a steep mountainside, the Japan of old could be seen in a post-and-beam Japanese farmhouse surrounded by terraced rice fields.

When the train pulled into Fuji City, Hoglund climbed out onto the platform and looked around. The office buildings and department stores across from the train station looked an awful lot like those in Tokyo. Fuji City might be a mill town surrounded by mountains and a bay, but that was where the comparison with Port Angeles stopped. The words used to describe his home—isolated, rustic, sleepy—certainly didn't apply here.

Like Port Angeles, Fuji City is a slave to its geography, to its proximity to the ocean and Japan's most famous physical landmark, the mountain that has been immortalized in Japanese woodblock prints and haiku. But where Port Angeles exists as an adjunct to the physical drama that unfolds around it, Fuji City's dramatic physical attributes take second place to the business of making money. In just three miles, there are more than three hundred paper mills of various sizes, leaving the skyline a collage of boxes and smokestacks. On a good day, when the air over the city isn't filled with a haze of gray smoke, Mount Fuji can be seen silhouetted against the sky, a picturesque backdrop to a picture of industrial efficiency.

In recent years, the Saito family has dominated the region. While Daishowa's corporate headquarters are now in Tokyo, the company's origins—and its soul—are in Fuji City. Daishowa operates three large mills in the Fuji region, the largest of which employs more than a thousand people, and reaps the benefit of personal and political ties that extend all the way to the Japanese Diet (parliament) Building, in the center of Tokyo. Shigeyoshi Saito, the younger brother of Ryoei Saito, is the governor of Shizuoka Province, where Fuji City is located. Toshitsugu, Ryoei's son and fellow Daishowa director, holds the same seat in the lower house of the parliament his uncle held before moving to the governorship. And the family influence has been extended by marriage, according to *The Wall Street Journal*. Shigeyoshi married the sister of Toyota Motor Corp.'s president, Shoichiro Toyoda. One of Ryoei's sons married the niece of former prime minister Yasuhiro Nakasone; another married into the family that controls Bridgestone Corp., the huge rubber and tire company.

Few dare to criticize Fuji City's cash cow and corporate provider. Two decades ago, a Japanese businessman named Matsugu Kasai helped organize antipollution rallies in Fuji City. Hundreds of people gathered near the bay waving banners and were joined by disgruntled fishermen who complained about the impact of the pollution on the fish population. The agitation reached all the way to the parliament, which eventually passed tougher environmental laws against industrial polluters.

Buoyed by the success of his campaign, Kasai ran for a city council seat against a candidate supported by Daishowa. After winning a seat on the Fuji City Council, the former employee of Japan Express, a transportation company, continued his fight against industrial pollution by Daishowa and other major paper companies. But one is far more likely to find Daishowa supporters than critics in Fuji City government offices, which benefit handsomely from Daishowa's contributions to the tax base and its educational programs. People had come to assume that what was good for Daishowa was good for the community.

●   ●   ●

AS A HOUSE FATHER FOR the Daishowa baseball team, Keiji Okawa was used to baby-sitting some high-strung personalities. In a company of workhorses, his twenty-seven young men were thoroughbreds. Their work at the office—usually pushing paper across a desk—was secondary to winning baseball games. Okawa's job was keeping them well fed, well rested, and out of trouble. He and his wife, Chizuko, were in charge of the dormitory where team members spent their time when they weren't at work, practicing, or playing games.

Baseball in Japan is a marketing phenomenon, where teams sponsored by department stores, beer companies, and trading companies are used as advertising tools and morale boosters. When Daishowa's team won the national championships in 1980, the city made them heroes, and they lived—by Japanese standards—accordingly.

But for the next three weeks, Okawa had something bigger to worry about than his baseball team. Their names were Hoglund, Bryant, Adamich, and Hallman. In the fall of 1988, construction crews had been brought in to tear down the walls in the lounge where the baseball team watched television and relaxed. Some of the glass cases filled with trophies, photos, and other mementos were taken out; a small cooking facility with a refrigerator was added. New furniture was installed. The liquor cabinet was stocked with whiskey and sake, and a pink oversized telephone, similar to the ones that line the hallways in Japanese train stations, was put in one corner.

The four dormitory rooms next door to the lounge—each of which previously housed three team players—were enlarged, painted, and carpeted. Each room was provided with a sink, a miniature refrigerator, and an expensive wooden desk and closet. On each door, the remodelers hung a nameplate engraved with Japanese characters representing good luck or happiness. Down the hall, a bathroom was remodeled and a showerhead installed too high on the wall for the average Japanese.

Okawa had heard that some Americans liked Japanese food and could even use chopsticks, but he wasn't going to take any chances. He stocked the refrigerator in the lounge with luncheon meat, cheese, white bread, peanut butter, and lots of Kirin beer. By the time Daishowa officials were finished remodeling the dormitory just for the three-week visit of their four American visitors, the total bill came close to three hundred thousand dollars.

When the Americans arrived at the baseball team dormitory, they were immediately hustled into a meeting with the mill manager and then to a fitting session for their uniforms: white coveralls with their names embroidered across the pockets. Hallman hated the uniform because it made him feel like a car mechanic. But when it arrived the next day, a perfect fit, he put it on without protest. Since their arrival in Japan, the company had spent thousands of dollars entertaining them. It didn't seem right to refuse something as trivial as putting on a pair of overalls.

They were paired up—Hoglund and Hallman, Adamich and Bryant—and assigned to two different paper machines. Their agenda: to attend meetings, tour the company's three mills, and spend time observing and working with their counterparts from Japan. It was, by Port Angeles standards, easy work. But since their arrival in Japan, the only thing that seemed easy was falling asleep—and that was after they got used to pillows that felt like cement blocks.

In many ways, Daishowa's Fuji mill was not so different from what they had left behind in Port Angeles. The Japanese even used some English words for certain parts or processes— a product of the internationalization of the industry. The company's numbers provided some interesting comparisons: The average employee at the Fuji mill was forty-one years old and earned $40,000 to $50,000 a year, including overtime. All employees were automatically enrolled in the company union and paid monthly dues of 2 to 3 percent of wages. Housing costs were high—$400,000 for a typical three-bedroom house—and most of the employees commuted at least one hour to work each day.

In Port Angeles, the average salary of a millworker was about $56,000 a year. But living costs were significantly lower than in Japan, since most Port Angeles workers lived within a few miles of the mill and the average home cost about $75,000 in 1990.

On his first day in the mill, Hoglund was shocked to see

that the computers being used were an older version of those in the mill back home. He had heard so much about the high-tech successes of the Japanese that he had come expecting to see R2D2, the robot from *Star Wars*, running the paper machines.

But that was one of those contradictions Hoglund learned to accept, if not understand, after a few days in Japan. The modern skyscraper next to the tiny wooden shrine dating back several centuries. Blocks of shops with the latest in electronic gadgets—television watches, high-definition television, bread-making machines—and banks filled with dozens of employees performing a job done by one person and a computer back home. An almost religious devotion to the idea of a traditional nuclear family was juxtaposed against bars filled with fathers and husbands drinking into the small hours of the morning. It would be these things the four papermakers would puzzle over in their off hours, when they shared a Kirin beer from their private refrigerator.

Working with the machines was something Hoglund enjoyed because he could usually figure out how to operate them, based on his knowledge of the papermaking process. Communicating with people was much more frustrating. He would sit in meetings with the Japanese managers and feel trapped. It was difficult to use sign language and gestures when they were talking about a technical process. Often, he would say something and get a room full of blank stares. He was never sure whether they really understood him, even though they nodded as if in agreement. After a while, he realized that he was nodding in response even when he didn't understand them. It began to feel as if he were surrounded by dialogue where none really existed.

At times, the communication gulf was a bottomless chasm that no amount of good humor could overcome. Time and time again, the American papermakers ended up feeling like inarticulate children. Each of them confronted their frustrations differently. Hallman, a quiet man who hated asking a question more than once, started putting tape on all the buttons of the machines and scribbling their names in English. Bryant, who had enrolled in Japanese language classes at the community college back home, brought along his Japanese language dictionary and tried out some of his elementary phrases on his Japanese coworkers. When all else failed, Adamich tried cracking jokes. Often they fell flat on their Japanese audience, but the good-faith effort sometimes helped break the tension.

At first, Hoglund just did what he was told—or what he thought he was told. When things got slow on the paper machine and someone handed him a paintbrush and a can of paint, he took it. At the end of the day, when someone handed him a broom, he took it too. But several days into their stay in Fuji City, Hoglund began to feel like he was a nineteen-year-old rookie again, shoveling sawdust in his father's shadow. He was spending more time with a paintbrush and a broom than the paper machine. This just didn't seem right. One day, he and Hallman were splashing paint on a piece of equipment and grumbling to themselves. "We didn't come thousands of miles to do this, to do someone's grunt work. What are we doing here?" Just at that moment, a Japanese employee came out of the break room and looked over at them. Hoglund was sure he saw a smirk on his face as he walked past. "If I had the balls, I'd pack it up and go home," he told Hallman, so angry he could barely get the words out.

After a long day on the mill floor, Hoglund's inclination was to retreat to the lounge, grab a beer, and watch something on television that didn't require a lot of thought. If only for a few moments, immersed in reruns of bad American television sitcoms or Japanese baseball, he could feel connected to a world that he understood.

Adamich and Bryant were curious to see what life was like outside the mill gate. At first, when they began exploring Fuji City on their own, they relied on some pieces of paper provided by the company. They were instructions for cab drivers, one side written in English and the other in Japanese. "Could you take me to the grocery store?" "Could you take me to the Fuji mill?" But after a few days, they figured out which direction to take downtown and began exploring the city on foot.

It was in the streets of Fuji City, away from the gaze of their Japanese coworkers, that the Americans collected their tales of modern Japanese culture. Everywhere they went, the two men were treated with extreme, almost embarrassing, politeness. There were countless times when strangers or people from the mill went out of their way to help them navigate the unfamiliar turf.

One Sunday, an elderly Japanese shopkeeper closed down his shop to guide them to the local Mormon church so Hallman could attend the service. Another weekend, a Daishowa supervisor took them on a day trip to Mount Fuji. In the evenings, some of the young baseball players would come into the lounge and drink beer or watch television, at least until the night they got too rowdy and were banished to their half of the dormitory. Every day at noon, some of the Japanese papermakers would bring out new delicacies for their guests to sample: pickled vegetables; rice balls wrapped in seaweed; marinated fish.

On the culinary front, Bryant was the most adventurous. Adamich ate some sushi, but never developed a liking for raw tuna, sea urchin, or sturgeon eggs. Hoglund, on the other hand, limited his gourmet experiments to things he could recognize, with a decided preference for sukiyaki, noodles, and Kirin beer.

Outside the earshot of their supervisors, the Japanese had their own questions for their American visitors. What kind of a car do you drive? How big is your house? How much money do you make? One young man who was about to get married told them that his salary would be increased because he was taking on family obligations. Others complained about living in cramped quarters in the company dormitory because they couldn't afford to buy a house even after working two decades in the mill.

Much of what the Americans heard from the Japanese seemed familiar: Housing was too expensive, good schools for their children were tough to find, and their jobs were too "stomach-hurting." One big difference between the Americans and their Japanese friends was the attitude toward vacations. As senior mill employees, the four Port Angeles men enjoyed six or seven weeks of vacation a year, which they used religiously for hunting, fishing, or working on the house. The Japanese papermakers, who earned a week's vacation after three years of employment, complained about not knowing how to enjoy their leisure time. Often, they didn't even take off more than three or four days at a time.

But every step of the way, from the moment they got up for breakfast in the dormitory to lights out at night, there were reminders that they were far from home. Little things started to get irritating because they were adding up, one after another, into something big.

For Hoglund, it was the pressures to conform that bothered him the most, daily reminders of the dangers of individual expression in a society based on the group. In the mill, that sense of sameness began with the morning exercises and ended with sweeping the floor. Everyone—from the paper-machine supervisor to the most junior hire—took part. But to Hoglund, seniority meant not having to sweep the floors. America's heroes—whether they were log-cabin presidents, high-flying astronauts, or billionaires—were people who had worked their way out of doing the menial work.

Loneliness also took a toll on the Port Angeles men, especially Hoglund. He missed Marcy and the kids even more than he had expected. He missed hearing his wife talk about the people she had met at the grocery store, where she worked as a cashier and bookkeeper. He missed the calls home from Steven, who had started experiencing his own version of homesickness after leaving to attend college classes in Bellingham, across Puget Sound from Port Angeles. Hoglund still had a tough time admitting that his son was so far away; it was like losing his best friend and hunting buddy at the same time.

There was the phone, although he didn't want to abuse the long-distance privileges. He tried to call home every three or four days. And Marcy wrote every other day because she could tell from the phone calls that her husband needed news from home.

•   •   •

THE EDGE OF THE ENVELOPE was slit open from end to end and then taped. There was no attempt to hide the fact that someone had opened, and possibly read, what was supposed to be a private letter from a wife to a husband. There was nothing written on the letter to indicate that the person had made a mistake and was feeling apologetic. How could anyone, even a Japanese secretary unschooled in the correspondence of foreigners, fail to see that this letter addressed to him in English was a piece of personal correspondence?

Unless, of course, it wasn't a mistake at all.

The longer Hoglund held the letter from Marcy, the madder he got. It was as if someone had walked into his mind without asking. In Japan, the company might own a person's loyalty, his time, and even, perhaps, his mail. But not in America.

Hoglund approached one of the Japanese millworkers and asked him why his mail was opened. In broken English, the man replied, "It went to the wrong address, and they had to look inside to find out where it should go." Look inside? Hoglund felt confused and trapped, tired of feeling awkward and stupid, too big to fit into the seats, too boisterous to feel comfortable, too concerned about doing the wrong thing, whatever that might be.

Hoglund wanted to go home. Not in ten days, but tomorrow. Several hours later, the four papermakers from Port Angeles stood in the lounge of the dormitory. Adamich and Bryant argued against jumping ship. They were halfway through their trip to Japan, and the reputation of their mill, and its American workers, was on the line. They thought it was probably just an overzealous secretary. Adamich, who blamed the whole thing on a bad case of homesickness, thought Hoglund was blowing things way out of proportion. He was a little embarrassed by all the attention they had gotten from the company, especially those fancy rooms, and thought it was unfair to put their hosts in such an awkward position. But Hallman was on Hoglund's side. His stomach still hurt, and he wanted to go back to Alyce, his three teenage girls, and a doctor who spoke his language.

Bryant could see Hoglund and Hallman were close to reaching their personal point of no return. And he shared some of their discomfort, especially the daily confirmation that their assignment was to become converts to the Japanese way. Adamich kept arguing that going home early was an admission of failure, but Bryant began to weaken. If two of them went, they all should go.

Bryant phoned their supervisor, Henry Smedley. "We've got a problem," he said. "Things are falling apart. You've got to bring us home." The message went up the line from Smedley to Dave Tamaki to Mochizuki and back to the people in Fuji City and Tokyo. The Americans wanted out.

While phone calls bounced back and forth across the Pacific, Hoglund sat in the break room and talked with a young papermaker named Masayuki Akita. It was the way he dealt with stressful situations: to blow off steam and then move on. Now that he was past the explosion, it was time to try to figure things out.

Akita, an outgoing young man with ambitions of a career overseas, spoke English better than most of his coworkers. He tried to explain to Hoglund how the mail system at the mill worked. All the mail that went into the mill office was opened by a young secretary and placed on the mill manager's desk to read. Since his letter had gone to the main mill, rather than to the dormitory, it slipped into a pile that was automatically opened.

Once it was explained to him, Hoglund felt foolish.

When the conversation turned to the proposed mill expansion in Port Angeles, Akita asked why the union was so concerned that any new jobs go to union employees. Hoglund explained to the young Japanese papermaker that Americans needed labor unions because they didn't have a system like Japan's where the company was expected to take care of its employees like a family. The Port Angeles mill—with three owners over a two-year period—was an example of how little loyalty American companies had for their employees. In Hoglund's view, a company was there for the good times, but a union would be there forever.

As he became more comfortable with Akita, who was about his son's age, Hoglund worked up the nerve to express his frustration about the trip. Why was he painting equipment instead of running the paper machines? What was the point?

"You're not here to learn how to make paper," he recalled Akita telling him. "You're here to learn our system."

"Of course," Hoglund thought to himself. "Why hadn't somebody just come out weeks earlier and said that?"

By the time the phone rang, Hoglund had most of his questions answered. Mochizuki was on the line. From his side of the Pacific, the questions were just beginning.

•   •   •

MOCHIZUKI KNEW, without anyone telling him, that the failure of this trip would be the end of his career in Port Angeles. For the people in Tokyo, the crisis had become a test of his leadership. He knew the questions that were being asked: "Why was his management so bad? Why had he selected these four men?" In Tokyo, a failure of this magnitude, with this

much public exposure, would require a "very serious" response. He was sure they would send over a large team of
Japanese managers to take control of the mill.

When Hoglund came on the line, Mochizuki apologized
for the letter being opened and once again explained the mail
system at the Fuji mill. He said he would work hard to make
the rest of their stay better, including finding a way to overcome the language problems. "But if you come home it will
be a serious problem," he told the American papermaker.
"You must stay."

Hoglund, increasingly sensitive to the repercussions of his
personal revolt, agreed to stay put. With every conversation,
he felt more embarrassed. The next morning, Teruo Kondo
and another Daishowa official from Tokyo got on a train to
Fuji City. When they arrived at the mill, the four papermakers
were called into one of the meeting rooms. "What do you
want?" they asked the Americans.

By the meeting's conclusion, the Daishowa officials had
agreed to put Hallman on a plane back home and move Hoglund onto the same work crew as Bryant and Adamich. Masayuki Akita, who came to be known as Masa, was assigned to
be their full-time shadow, interpreter, cultural attaché, and
friend.

For Hoglund, the crisis was over. But the impact of his
single act of defiance was not. Daishowa officials asked the
secretary who had accidentally opened his letter to apologize
personally to the American millworker. But Hoglund really
didn't want a "sweet little office gal" to suffer so much for a
simple misunderstanding, so he told them an apology was
unnecessary.

•   •   •

THE DAY BEFORE their departure, Adamich, Bryant, and Hoglund were brought to a conference room in Fuji City with the mill manager, the paper-machine supervisor, and several others who had worked with them during their three-week stay. It was, in keeping with the tradition of corporate Japan, a formal event. The incident with the letter had cleared the air but had also left some raw nerves on both sides. With Masa's help, the last week had gone a lot more smoothly. The Americans had settled into being tourists. They shopped for souvenirs. They participated in a company sports day, complete with a three-legged race and track events. Now, as they stood in that room surrounded by their Japanese coworkers, they knew this was their final opportunity to speak their minds.

Adamich, who, as the senior member of the group, spoke first, told them he had seen a tremendous improvement in the country since his visit as a young navy man. He thanked them for their hospitality. And then he told them that the things that worked in Japan simply couldn't be transplanted to the mill in Port Angeles.

"In your country everyone is the same, and you are brought up to believe the same things and work together," he said. "In America, we have many different kinds of people, and everyone thinks very differently."

As the conversation unfolded, the Port Angeles papermakers admitted there was room for improvement back home. But not on the level their hosts envisioned. Hoglund liked the way the Japanese workers organized their equipment. Bryant was impressed with the meetings the Japanese paper-machine su-

pervisors held at the beginning and end of each shift to alert
the incoming crew to any peculiarities experienced with the
machines during the past eight hours. But it was clear by the
end of the meeting that the Americans, while friendly, were
not converts to the Daishowa way. They had come to Japan
three weeks earlier, convinced of the American way. And they
were leaving even more so, having seen the underpinnings of
Japanese society that supported Daishowa's management style
in Japan.

When the meeting concluded, there was another round of
thanks. It was gracious and cordial, smiles and handshakes. If
the Daishowa officials were disappointed, they didn't show it.
That night, the Americans enjoyed a lavish sukiyaki dinner at
a restaurant in downtown Fuji City. It was, by their memories,
a festive occasion buoyed by a certain sense of relief on the
part of both sides that the whole thing was over. The Port
Angeles crew were ready to go home, and their hosts were
ready to be freed of their obligations.

Hitachi Wakamiko, a paper-machine supervisor who was
an amateur photographer, gave them each a signed photo of
Mount Fuji. There was toast after toast, to friendship and
mutual respect. There was lots of laughter. They drank a lot
of beer and sake and ate very well. Sometime during the
dinner, which Hoglund remembers as the "best meal I've
ever had," he found himself desperately trying to understand
something one of his Japanese friends was asking. In his frustration, Hoglund finally handed him a piece of paper and a
pen. The friend scribbled for a minute and handed it back to
Hoglund. There, on the paper, was the question written in
perfect English. The Japanese worker could read and write
the language better than many Americans. "All that time I had

been struggling and I could have just handed them a piece of paper and a pencil," Hoglund thought to himself.

From there, the group progressed to a bar where they continued drinking beer and sake and became increasingly philosophical. At one point, one of the Japanese supervisors grabbed the buttocks of one of the young female office workers as she strolled past. "You better not do that in America, or you will be in big trouble," Adamich warned his new friend.

There was more beer and sake. Adamich and Bryant—at the urging of their friends—got up and sang. It hadn't taken them too long to figure out that in the world of *karaoke*, tonal quality was not as important as a good attitude. But even the warm feelings and alcohol weren't enough to persuade Hoglund to get out of his seat and in front of a microphone.

By the time the four papermakers reached Fairchild International Airport in Port Angeles, they were beyond exhaustion. The late-night revelry, the train ride from Fuji City to Narita Airport, and the long plane ride home had sapped any remaining energy from their bodies. All they wanted was to see their wives and children and find a comfortable bed. The next afternoon, still suffering from jet lag, they were called into a conference room at the mill for a debriefing with Mochizuki, Tamaki, Smedley, and several others. Hoglund noticed they all had a copy of a fax in front of them. Later, he realized it was the notes from the Daishowa officials at the Fuji City meeting.

"What do you think about what you saw?" Mochizuki asked them.

"The quality of people over here is better than the quality of the people over there," Adamich told them.

The room was silent.

"Was there anything you learned over there that could be used in Port Angeles?" they were asked.

Bryant mentioned the Japanese tradition of meeting right before a new shift starts. But his boss, Smedley, said that couldn't be done in Port Angeles because the union would demand overtime if they asked the crews to come in five minutes early.

Over and over, in different ways, the four papermakers emphasized their feeling that the Japanese system wouldn't work for Americans. It was the paper machines, not the people, that were better in Japan, they told their bosses. Provide us with the best equipment and we can compete with anyone.

The meeting sounded a lot like the one in Fuji City. The same questions. The same polite, but occasionally defiant, responses. Mochizuki returned to his office dejected, convinced the trip was a big, costly mistake. Hallman, who had been checked by his doctor and given a clean bill of health upon his return, was the only one who expressed enthusiasm for the feeling of "family" that Daishowa cultivated among its employees. The others seemed to have been pushed even further into their conviction that their way was right. The face-off between corporate Japan and blue-collar America looked like a stalemate.

III.

THE EVENTS THAT CONSPIRED to break the stalemate between the Port Angeles millworkers and their Japanese managers were not the kind of things that would end up in newspaper articles or history books. If they were revealed at all, it would be more likely to happen over a cup of coffee or a schooner of beer. They were either too insignificant or too personal to share, except, perhaps, as a conversational aside.

In the weeks following their return from Japan, Hoglund and the other three papermakers kept waiting for a call from the front office requesting their help, something that would justify their three-week stint as very expensive guinea pigs. A few of the guys asked Hoglund some questions about Japan. But only one supervisor even bothered to ask about the trip. It was as if the visit to Japan had never happened at all. They got out of bed, went to work, and did the same job with the same people in the same way they had done it before. Or at least it seemed that way for a while.

Hoglund didn't really think about it, but some of the things he used to write off as cultural differences didn't seem quite as simple anymore. A tidy guy by nature, he soon got tired of stumbling over the overalls and other gear that inevitably piled up next to his machine. It was more than irritating—it was dangerous and expensive. When the paper machine got shut down for repair, the crew was under pressure to get it going again as quickly as possible. Every minute lost because of injuries or misplaced tools translated into thousands of dollars of unsold paper.

In Japan, the crew kept their tools and rain gear in a cabinet next to the paper machine. Hoglund asked his supervisor whether he could get a similar system at the number three paper machine. But even after a metal cabinet was made available, he couldn't persuade his colleagues to put their tools away. People tended to drop their tools at the spot where they used them and hang their raingear over the nearest pipe. After a while, he gave up asking.

Hoglund and the other papermakers were being asked to

take on more responsibility for the quality and quantity of the paper that was leaving their mill. The pulp and paper market was in trouble—too much product chasing too few dollars—and that increased the pressure to do things faster and better. If the printing plant in California had a problem with the paper off the number three machine, Hoglund and his coworkers heard about it immediately and were expected to try to find a solution.

When the company embarked on a twenty-two-million-dollar rebuild of the number three paper machine in early 1989, Hoglund and Adamich were put on a team of employees assigned to draw up a training manual. For six months, Hoglund spent his days studying the new machinery and trying to transfer his understanding of the system into words. At night, he would come home with paper and pencils and draw diagrams to match the pictures in his mind. In the past, he'd always just concentrated on his piece of the puzzle. Now he was being forced mentally to dissect and re-create the entire process from pulp to paper roll, an exercise that made it easier for him to pinpoint problems. He felt proud when he heard that some outsiders were asking for copies of the safety manual.

The extra responsibilities had their rewards. For the first time in thirty years with the mill on Ediz Hook, Hoglund got his own office. It wasn't anything fancy—a small room with a desk, a chair, a file cabinet, and a coffee machine. When he ran out of coffee or filters, he went to the main storeroom and got some more. In the old days, before Daishowa, he would never have gotten coffee from the company, at least not with the knowledge of his supervisor.

In the big world of labor-management relations, a free cup

of coffee is a small thing. But often it is the profusion of small things that add up to an overall good or bad feeling. Under Crown Zellerbach and even James River, millworkers complained that the goodwill was limited to the terms of the labor contract. Extra benefits were distributed at the discretion of the individual managers, and rarely did the thank yous extend beyond a cup of coffee and doughnuts at a morning meeting. After Daishowa took over the mill, there was a noticeable shift in the management's treatment of its union workers. When managers held safety meetings with their crews, they brought in sandwiches and salad. Birthdays were recognized with a card and a couple of movie passes.

Hoglund's major complaint was the pressure to improve. After a good day, he wanted to go home, have a beer, and watch some television. But without fail, his boss would come back the next day from the meeting with Mochizuki, loaded up with new areas for improvement. It was relentless, a steep stairway with no end in sight. More than anything else, this *kaizen*, or continuous refinement, was a source of frustration for Hoglund and his fellow crew members. "You just can't please them," he often thought to himself.

Hoglund wasn't the only one to find the ground shifting after his return to Port Angeles. Bryant, the young president of AWPPW's Local 169, came home to more snide remarks about selling out to the enemy. His critics seemed far less concerned about what he had learned about the Daishowa style of management than about the fact that he had gotten a free trip and some nice meals. He still considered himself a union man but decided it was time to think about getting out of union politics and concentrate on his work and family.

Hallman, a man who rarely showed emotions about anything, would light up when he told friends about his trip to Mount Fuji and the sense of family he saw at Daishowa's Fuji City mill. In the basement of his house, Hallman had a hobby room where he kept his tools and outdoor gear. On the wall, he hung the picture of Mount Fuji given to him at the end of his trip. He was not a man to brag about anything, but his wife, Alyce, noticed he often showed that picture to friends when they came to visit.

Over time, the trip to Japan began to sound better and better: the lavish meals, the endless Kirin beer, the trip to Mount Fuji, and the friendship of the Japanese papermakers. Each time the four American papermakers told the stories to friends or family, Daishowa's generosity seemed to expand.

One day, Hoglund grew curious about the gifts he and the other three papermakers had received in Japan from Daishowa, including a 35-millimeter camera and a silk scarf for their wives. At the time, he had assumed the camera was an inexpensive model, the kind you might get free for ordering a magazine subscription. Out of curiosity, he called a local camera store and asked for the price. He was shocked. It cost more than two hundred dollars.

•   •   •

In June 1989, Daishowa had a string of bad news. Three weeks after its contract expired with the AWPPW, the company called off its $560-million mill expansion because of the uncertainty over wood-chip supplies, the steep slide of the value of the dollar against the yen, the weakness in the global pulp market, and delays with environmental permits. The official word was a postponement of at least a year, but most community leaders resigned themselves to a future without a million-dollar addition to the Port Angeles tax base.

Propelled by a powerful "Take back the land" movement, the heated battle to remove the Elwha River dams was shifting to the political arena. Two Democratic politicians—Senator Brock Adams and Representative Al Swift—were trying to negotiate a legislative solution to the complicated legal battle that would allow the removal of the dams and still guarantee clean water for Port Angeles and low-cost power for the paper mill. In Congress, where Japanese investment was a flashpoint for high-profile flag-waving, Daishowa couldn't risk being depicted as a rich foreigner putting American workers on the picket line.

As tensions mounted over the contract, there were rumors on the mill floor about getting tough with union-busting Japanese companies. Mochizuki was worried the union planned to hang Daishowa out to dry, playing on its vulnerability as a rich foreign company to jack up the contract so other American companies would have to follow suit. Over the summer, the negotiating team met thirty-eight times, starting out in a room above the swimming pool in Aggie's Motel before they were forced to move into another cheap motel because of the chlorine fumes.

Mochizuki desperately wanted to stanch the drain on morale by getting a contract. To avoid the "no, no, yes" style of negotiation—in which both sides spend countless hours wading through unreasonable demands in the hope of getting something close to their bottom line—he did something unheard of in the history of the AWPPW. According to union negotiators, Daishowa gave them the company's bottom line, including how many millions of dollars it was willing to spend over a five-year period, and asked them to decide whether to spend it on pensions, wage hikes, or other benefits.

After many heated arguments, the union negotiating team ended up taking away the employer's contribution to the 401(k) retirement plan—a popular program started under James River—and added that money to pensions and wages. Norm Weekes, the union's chief negotiator, argued that the retirement benefits were great for the older workers but didn't put money in the pockets of the newer employees.

The AWPPW, in effect, had become part of the solution— or part of the problem, depending on your perspective. By turning over the responsibility for divvying up the money to the union, Daishowa had also given it the job of selling the contract to its 241 members. The following week, the negotiating team took the contract to the local and recommended acceptance. It was a five-year contract that granted each member a sixteen-hundred-dollar payment upon ratification of the contract and an 11.75 percent raise spread over the remaining four years. Daishowa estimated the contract to be worth an additional sixty-one million dollars in wages and benefits over the five-year period.

On the union side, there was a lot of grumbling about the loss of the employer's contributions to the 401(k) plan, a benefit that would still be received by managers. But Hoglund, like many others, wasn't angry enough to vote no. They needed their jobs and finally had some that just might outlast them. Pension plans and long-term contracts meant a lot more from a company that looked like it would be in business for a while. The vote was 72–28 percent in favor of accepting the contract.

A five-year contract was a reason for celebration in the Hoglund household. They could start looking for a new pickup truck. And Hoglund could hardly wait to get out to his friend's cabin on Lake Ozette, just a few miles from the beach where the Japanese sailors had washed ashore so long ago. His annual hunting trip with his son Steven was his favorite vacation of the year, and he'd wasted too many hunting seasons worrying about how he was going to pay his bills during a strike.

Mochizuki was also planning a celebration. In exchange for a healthy wage increase, the company had achieved a long-term contract and flexible job classifications in the machine shop, so one employee could handle several jobs if necessary. That type of work structure, similar to the one witnessed by the papermakers in Japan, was a top priority for Daishowa. Once it was introduced to the Port Angeles mill, Mochizuki believed it would only be a matter of time before he would be able to spread those ideas to the rest of the mill. He was convinced, in the same way the Christian missionaries in Japan were convinced about their unbelievers, that the union would eventually be won over to the Daishowa way.

(In fact, the union sorely underestimated the popularity of the flexible job classifications opposed in theory by Hoglund and some of the other Port Angeles papermakers. Since it was voluntary—any of the electricians, pipe fitters, or welders could choose to move into the multicraft classification for higher pay—the union predicted there would be just a couple of takers. Instead, nearly all of the machine-shop employees elected to become multicraft workers, including Bryant, who moved over from the paper machine when there was an opening.)

Mochizuki arranged a luncheon at the Downrigger, a restaurant overlooking the waterfront, and invited Weekes, the union's chief negotiator, to join him for a contract-signing celebration. Usually these things were a perfunctory operation performed in someone's office with a signature and a handshake. Weekes knew a lot of union members would consider him a sellout, but he didn't think his ethics were compromised by a free meal.

Weekes was glad he wore a suit, since a photographer attended the luncheon to commemorate the moment when the pens touched the paper. Aside from a few brief business meetings, Weekes had never really held a conversation with Mochizuki. As the meal drew to a close, Weekes turned to the Japanese mill manager and said, "I hope you're satisfied with the outcome of the contract."

"No, not really," was Mochizuki's reply.

Weekes was shocked. He was under the impression Daishowa was happy with the contract. When he pressed Mochizuki further, it became clear that the problem was not really the contract. Daishowa tradition was that its managers stayed at an overseas posting until the contract ran out and a new one began. But after spending more than two decades at the beck and call of the men in Daishowa's Tokyo office, Mochizuki, who had once dreaded the move to America, was already starting to dread the inevitable call home.

Freed of the obligations of extended family and corporation that are part of Japanese society, he and Fumiko had begun to fashion a life of their own. In addition to attending company functions together, something that rarely happened in Japan, they played golf in the evenings, went to dinner with friends, and had even fitted in a couple of family ski trips to Oregon's Mount Bachelor, and Whistler, the well-known resort north of Vancouver, British Columbia.

Back home, Mochizuki wouldn't socialize outside of work with the rank and file on a regular basis. A person raised in Japan would understand the risks of too much familiarity between a boss and subordinate outside the company and the penalties that exist for those who violate the boundaries. But as part of his effort to close the gap between the management and the union, he started up two annual company golf tournaments that were open to everyone. Spouses were invited to company awards dinners and were sometimes invited to the out-of-town meetings with customers.

Mochizuki even spent every Monday night at the Port Angeles Lanes with the mill's bowling team, dusting off his twenty-year-old bowling ball from college. When Fumiko balked at joining the "Head Pins," he told her it was her responsibility to participate in a very "American" pastime.

Daishowa also was working hard to leave its imprint on Port Angeles: donating thirty-six thousand dollars to the city to complete a Little League field; sponsoring the city's hundredth birthday celebration; purchasing high-tech equipment for Olympic Memorial Hospital; and buying a table at a wine-tasting reception to raise money for the hospice program. The company's budget for charitable donations more than doubled, while fund-raising became yet another form of friendly competition. Divisions within the company were encouraged to try to outdo each other in the annual United Way campaign. Mochizuki and Fumiko, dressed in the distinctive blue Daishowa jackets that were distributed to employees, led the company's delegation in the annual March of Dimes walkathon along the Port Angeles waterfront.

Increasingly, the Mochizukis found themselves childless. Makoto's love of sports, particularly football, drew him right into the center of Peninsula High School activities. When the University of Washington's football team went to the Rose Bowl, he was there in the stands with his best friend's family. His interest in the competitive psyche extended beyond high school sports. Instead of talking about returning to Japan, he began looking into colleges in the United States that offered programs in sports medicine and psychology. As Akira's English improved, he also grew more adventurous. The first fall after his family moved to the United States, he returned to Japan for a vacation and discovered his friends consumed with cramming for the college entrance exams. His memories of his boyhood pals didn't match the realities of their "study, study, study" existence. When he returned to Port Angeles, he sent away for brochures from small private colleges in America.

Privately, the Mochizukis had considered something they would never dare tell their elderly parents or relatives back home. In their travels around the Northwest, they had begun fantasizing about the possibility of buying a retirement home in America. Putting down semipermanent roots in the U.S. was something people back in Japan would have a difficult time accepting.

A cushion of community acceptance couldn't always protect Mochizuki or the other Japanese employees from the consequences of their national affiliation. During good times, they were employers, neighbors, parents, and friends. During bad times, they were still Japanese. Mochizuki dreaded those mornings when his goodwill efforts were sabotaged by newspaper headlines trumpeting the latest fracture in the U.S.-Japan relationship: a Japanese politician's comments about blacks; a dispute over U.S. access to the Japanese semiconductor market; an allegation of unethical behavior by a Japanese company. More than once, in a supervisor's meeting, he found himself feeling compelled to explain why he didn't agree with a comment from some opinionated Japanese politician or businessman. But hostile looks or remarks from someone he met out in the community, a not-so-rare occurrence during the Mochizukis' first year in Port Angeles, were uncommon. And when the Japanese manager found himself on the receiving end of an aggressive stare, it was almost always from a stranger, someone who didn't really belong in this town that had carved out a place for him and his family.

In all his calculations about the risks of coming to America, Mochizuki had never considered the possibility that he might not want to leave.

• • •

ON MAY 5, 1990, HOGLUND WALKED out the door of the mill and got in his truck to drive home. He was dog-tired, as he usually was when he worked swing shift, but as he drove away from the mill he gazed out across the Strait of Juan de Fuca and was tempted. The water was unusually smooth, like a sheen of oil lying atop a blacktop road, and it looked like there might be some good fishing.

But Hoglund knew that his body needed sleep more than his psyche needed a couple of hours with a fishing rod. So he turned his pickup truck toward home and crawled into bed just when the rest of the city was getting up to enjoy a weekend of baseball and picnics and hiking.

When Hoglund woke up that afternoon, he drove downtown to meet his wife, Marcy. On the drive, he could see out his truck window that the weather had taken a bad turn. The smooth water had turned into a churning mass of choppy waves and whitecaps. The town was buzzing with talk of fishermen in distress, boats that may or may not have gotten caught too far out when the wind started picking up. Families were taking stock: calling friends, checking with restaurants, hoping that this was the day their angler chose a cup of coffee and eggs over a morning on the water.

By the time Hoglund got to work that night, the news was all over the mill. Hallman and Jim Calvin, a forty-seven-year-old employee in the shipping department, had gone out that morning to a spot called Coyote, about six or seven miles out into the strait. They hadn't been heard from since. The next morning, when Hoglund left the mill, he drove past the boat launch and saw Calvin's truck and trailer still sitting in the parking lot.

That day, a policeman delivered the bad news to Hallman's wife, Alyce. A search crew had recovered the bodies. Hallman had tied himself to the boat with a piece of rope attached to his wrist. Calvin was found strapped into his life jacket floating about one hundred yards off shore, near the mouth of Morse Creek. From the position of the bodies in the water, it looked like the men had gotten the boat into the mouth of the harbor and were making a final run to shore when the boat was swamped.

Four Port Angeles men died that weekend in a storm that

could easily have claimed a lot more. At the mill, they lowered the flag to half-mast as a tribute to their two coworkers. "We lost two brothers," a Daishowa employee told the *Peninsula Daily News.* "These guys that were lost, these were special people. They were good, responsible men and they're going to be missed."

Hallman and Calvin fished together and were buried together, in one of the biggest funerals the Church of Jesus Christ of Latter-day Saints had ever seen. The people filled the sanctuary, the foyer, and overflowed into the halls. They had come to mourn the loss of two men whose lives had touched many parts of the community in quiet ways. There were men who had worked next to them at the mill for decades, families who attended their church, and a small group of Japanese managers who knew Hallman as a hard worker with a weak stomach.

Alyce didn't know many of the people who came to mourn her husband. But when the men who had known him stood up and told their stories about the quiet man with a passion for the woods and the water, she laughed and cried right along with the rest of them. And afterward, when the crowd started to leave, she squeezed her way through to the foyer and stood around accepting handshakes and hugs and kisses.

It would be months, in fact more than a year, before Alyce was able to think beyond losing the man with whom she had spent her whole adult life. Deep down inside, she was still the sixteen-year-old girl he had married. She was angry and scared. How could he leave her alone with three strong-willed teenagers? In her effort to cleanse her mind of Leon, she also wiped out any reference to Daishowa. But twice, in the months after his death, she was reminded of her husband's employers. When the check arrived for Leon's death benefits, there was some extra money. She heard that Mochizuki had instructed his accountant to add to the final total.

A few months later, Alyce got a phone call from Tamaki, who had been transferred from Port Angeles to the company's office in Seattle. He said he had a videotape from a Seattle television crew that contained some footage of Hallman at work. He asked if she would like a copy. He also told her to call him if she ever needed anything. Through her husband's death, Alyce discovered she had a place in Daishowa's extended family. She had never had any occasion to test Crown Zellerbach or James River in that way. But based on her experience, she was glad she didn't have to.

●　●　●

A FEW WEEKS AFTER the funeral, Daishowa opened its doors to Port Angeles for the first time since purchasing the mill. Retired couples from nearby Sequim, high-school students, and families with children came to see the place where their relatives and friends went to work each day. Some came to see how paper is made. Others came as voyeurs, hoping to glimpse Ryoei Saito, the rich old man from Japan who had just made headlines around the world with his $160.6 million purchase of two paintings—van Gogh's *Portrait of Dr. Gachet*, and Renoir's *Au Moulin de la Galette*. Ryoei Saito, however, was not planning to attend. Many others just couldn't pass up an opportunity for a free meal.

For months, Mochizuki and his employees had been planning every detail of this open house. They had developed a self-guided tour and posted signs along the way to help explain the papermaking process, from the preparation of the stock to the rolling of the paper. The presence of Yomoji Saito made it a high-anxiety event. Would people come? Would the tents stand up to the fierce winds that occasionally blew off the strait? Would there be enough to eat? Of Ryoei Saito's three sons, Yomoji, a onetime exchange student at Seattle University, was the most comfortable playing the role of global entrepreneur. As the president of Daishowa International, and the fourth in line, he spent much of his time on airplanes visiting Daishowa's overseas operations and had a home in Seattle as well as Tokyo.

Mochizuki worried Yomoji Saito's appearance would be overshadowed by the controversy over his father's art purchases. But those fears were unfounded. While the record-breaking acquisitions were featured prominently in *The New York Times* and *The Washington Post*, both the *Peninsula Daily News* and the *Chronicle* downplayed the Saito art stories. Del Price, the editor of the weekly *Chronicle*, didn't even run the story because he believed the eccentricities of Daishowa's chairman had little relevance to his readers.

For a city suffering badly from cutbacks in timber revenues, Daishowa had much more interesting news. At a ceremony prior to the open house, Saito told the crowd of local dignitaries and paper-company executives that Daishowa was researching the use of recycled pulp in its telephone-directory paper in Port Angeles. Taniguchi, the executive vice president of Daishowa America, told the crowd that the Port Angeles mill was a "symbol of the past, present, and future of Daishowa America."

At the end of the weekend, Mochizuki declared the open house a success. By most counts, it was the biggest party in Clallam County's history, attracting more than six thousand people. Smitty's Restaurant—the king of the blue-plate special—catered the event and served up more than 6,000 hamburgers, 4,000 hot dogs, 4,000 brownies, 4,000 ice-cream bars, and a hundred 40-pound tanks of premixed soft drinks. Even mill critics went away impressed.

Two months later, Daishowa released its plans to build a forty-million-dollar recycling facility on vacant land between the mill and a lagoon at the base of the sand spit. When the plant opened in 1992, Daishowa would be the first company in the United States to produce telephone-directory paper using recycled pulp. The recycled pulp would provide at least 40 percent of the pulp required by the mill.

While other Olympic Peninsula timber towns were beating down the doors of Congress in search of federal funds to save them from extinction, Daishowa had helped ease Port Angeles off the endangered list. But the same week as its announcement of the recycling facility in Port Angeles, the company also quietly called off its plans to build a five-hundred-million-dollar pulp mill in Coos Bay, Oregon, a once thriving lumber town that now made its money off tourists instead of logs. Negotiations were also under way to sell to a Japanese trading company part of Daishowa's new five-hundred-million-dollar pulp plant in Peace River, Alberta.

Ryoei Saito was in trouble.

When Daishowa came to Port Angeles in 1988, it was Hoglund and his coworkers who were threatened by the dramatic growth in the Japanese economy. But in the spring of 1991, the bill was coming due for aggressive corporate players like Saito who had borrowed billions of dollars to finance several years of overseas expansion. Pulp and paper companies, egged on by the low price of imported logs and low interest rates, had dramatically expanded their capacity and pushed down prices. In the past, the Japanese government would have stepped in and helped the pulp and paper manufacturers by creating a cartel that could control production rates and boost prices. But the U.S. government was putting pressure on Japan to discontinue its practice of providing "administrative guidance" to its manufacturers on the grounds that it gave them an unfair advantage over U.S. firms.

In March 1991, Daishowa reported a pretax loss of ¥13.9 billion ($108 million) compared with a pretax profit of ¥19.1 billion ($159 million) the previous year. The company's debts were estimated at around ¥450 billion ($3.75 billion) compared with sales of ¥350 billion ($2.91 billion). A coalition of banks led by the Industrial Bank of Japan began tightening the screws, and the company announced its plans to implement a five-year debt-reduction plan focused on selling off land, stocks, and other assets.

All across the Daishowa empire—from Australia to Fuji City to Port Angeles—people wondered where the cuts would come. In the past, Hoglund would have been worried too. But every day, he drove past the bulldozers and construction crews working on the recycling plant. For the first time in his career, he felt confident his bosses were looking past their quarterly stock dividends. One-hundred-year-old Douglas firs were the past. Recycling was the future. All he had to do was measure the hefty bins of newspapers he and his neighbors hauled out to the street every week.

When Bryant saw the story on Daishowa's financial troubles

in the *Pulp and Paper Week*, he clipped it out and posted it on the union bulletin board down at the mill. But he didn't lose sleep over the news because he had watched the company pump too much money into the mill to close its doors. Even if Daishowa wanted to get rid of its Port Angeles mill, he figured the company would have to find another buyer.

After being jilted several times, these American papermakers had no reason to trust anything but money as a measurement of corporate commitment. The $125 million Daishowa had pumped into the mill, along with the $40 million that was going into the recycling facility, was an investment in their future.

•   •   •

WHEN THE SAITO FAMILY finally dropped the ax, in the fall of 1991, it wasn't on its mills in Port Angeles, Eden, Australia, or Quebec, Canada. In an ironic twist, the victim of the Japanese recession was Fuji City, the Saito family's ancestral home and the heart of the Japanese papermaking industry. Daishowa's Japanese millworkers were not alone. Under pressure to develop new sources of raw materials, lower their manufacturing costs, and expand their markets, many Japanese companies began shifting their manufacturing overseas in the last half of the 1980s and in the early 1990s.

The word went out that within five years, seven of the Fuji mill's paper machines and three of four coating machines would be shut down. In the land of lifetime employment, the company planned to shrink its work force from more than 1,000 to 350. Daishowa quietly began talking to potential buyers for a prime piece of property next to the Fuji City Shinkansen station.

While other Daishowa mills operated at a loss, the Port Angeles mill made a small profit. Unscheduled shutdowns, which cost the mill twenty thousand dollars in lost revenue over a twenty-four-hour period, dropped from four or five times a month to once every other month. Since taking over the mill, Daishowa America had expanded its share of the U.S. market from 20 percent to more than 30 percent.

It was a fitting marriage between a feisty company from Japan and a Northwest timber community looking for a future. Japan's second-largest paper company had come to America in search of timber and been caught up in a backlash against decades of greed and indifference to the limits of the natural world. In order to adjust to timber and energy restrictions prompted by efforts to protect the spotted owl and the salmon, Daishowa was bringing the knowledge it gained from the ruins of World War II.

If Mochizuki had stayed behind in Fuji City, he would have been in charge of dismantling a piece of Daishowa's history. If Daishowa hadn't purchased the Port Angeles mill, Hoglund might have been part of the last generation of mill-workers on Ediz Hook. Together, they were embarking on a path that they hoped would ensure a better future for themselves and their children. With some reluctance and a great deal of anxiety, these twenty-first-century pioneers on the western shore of America were adding another chapter to the complex tale of two powerful nations.

For Daishowa, a company governed by market forces far beyond the shores of Japan, the future was not at the base of Mount Fuji, the home of total quality control and lifetime employment. The future depended, at least in part, on an isolated peninsula on the westernmost edge of America.

Epilogue

IN A CORNER OF BECKY HALL'S CLASSROOM sits a shelf lined with the discards of contemporary Japanese life: the contents of a Tokyo garbage can carefully preserved as if it were a rare treasure. The stash includes empty boxes, bottles, and jars with eclectic names such as Pocari Sweat, a popular Japanese soft drink, and Golden Curry. They are treasured gifts from a land this Port Angeles teacher has only experienced through books and video.

In the middle of the room, a small group of Port Angeles

Senior High School students—a mass of sweatshirts, head-bands, and hormones—are clustered around a color television. On the screen, a brown hairless figure waddles to the refrigerator, where he takes out a beer and drinks it. He burps. The room erupts in laughter. Apparently, alien beings can entertain in any language.

The Japanese garbage collection and the copy of a Japanese-language version of the popular movie *E.T.: The Extra-Terrestrial* are a gift to Hall from the son of a Japanese businessman who runs a small sawmill in Port Angeles. It seems somehow fitting that these American teenagers are learning Japanese from a movie featuring an alien who drops into an average American suburb and befriends a small boy with his endearing habits and love of Reese's Pieces.

Nearly 160 years after three exotic strangers passed on their language to a young American named Ranald MacDonald, young Japanese are doing the same for a new generation of Americans. If interest in language is a barometer of cultural affinity, then Washington State and Japan are closely tied. In tiny towns tucked away in the farm belt of eastern Washington and the foothills of the Cascade Mountains, from deep in the Olympic rain forest to the near-desert plateaus that line the Columbia River, kids of all ages are learning Japanese, many of them via satellite. Programs through the University of Washington's Jackson School of International Studies, an institution dedicated to the foreign-policy interests of the late senator Henry M. Jackson, have cultivated a new group of specialists dedicated to the teaching of the Japanese language. In the shadow of Mount Rainier, the Japan America Society of Seattle runs a total-immersion Japanese-language summer camp where participants eat miso soup and rice for breakfast and do their shopping with yen.

For Hall, a slender, dark-haired woman who taught Spanish and French for more than a decade, the Japanese classes at Port Angeles High are a rare treat. Through a process of self-selection, the students who end up in her Japanese classes are consistently the best and brightest: the ones who make the honor roll, play first string on the football and basketball teams, and still find time to think about a future beyond adolescence.

But Hall has also come to realize that most of her students have not come to her because they like the sound of the language or share a deep fascination with Japanese theater or calligraphy. For most of them, the Japanese language, like typing and dictation for women in the 1950s, is a survival skill.

These teenagers have read the stories about the twenty-something generation: the first group in postwar America who cannot assume a better life than their parents; the first to be robbed of the post–World War II American dream of a big house in the suburbs, a new car every three years, and a job with promotions and pay increases to cover orthodontists, designer jeans, and vacations.

In a classroom conversation about the impact of Japanese investment in America, they talk about living in a country that has failed to prepare its youth for reality, a world where Japanese as well as English is the language of commerce, where the individual will have to make sacrifices for the public good, where Americans take pride in something other than military might.

Their anger is not too far beneath their fear, a shot of raw, undiluted emotion that carries more than a hint of disgust. "I don't think we care enough to be a contender," says Bill Henry, a sophomore who had been selected to travel to Japan the coming summer in a goodwill-ambassador program run by the state. "I don't think we work hard enough. I don't think enough Americans have those work-based feelings that they have in Japan. A lot of Americans wouldn't want to stay after work and go drinking with the boss."

The bell rings, turning great philosophers back into ordinary teenagers. Not until later, when they put in the requisite half-hour to hour of nightly homework that Japanese requires, will they be forced back into this world of linguistic challenges, where a culture of vagueness and class divisions attach societal obligations to even the most superficial relationships.

As the students squeeze out the door onto the walkway, Hall is left to mull over some of the fear and frustration that she hears from her students. On a personal level, Hall is convinced the Japanese presence in Port Angeles has expanded the borders of a town that often feels out of touch with the world portrayed on the evening news. Friends like the Mochizukis have been her short course in Japanese life, providing a coveted window into the thoughts and actions of everyday modern Japan.

But sometimes, in private, she wonders whether the benefits she enjoys are somehow diminishing America's economic strength. "Lots of people are real worried about the Japanese taking over," Hall says. "I teach Japanese, and even I worry about it. I don't want to be contributing to it. But I don't think not understanding will make things any better."

In her students' attitudes, Hall recognizes a view of Japan that is at once pragmatic and hopeful and scared. They are told—by their parents, the schools, the media—that they should be prepared to work in a borderless world where products will be globally created and sold, and employers will be judged by performance rather than their national origin. But the verdict is far from clear on just how this dramatic shift in economic and political power will affect their lives.

It is impossible to sit in Hall's Port Angeles Senior High School classroom and not feel as if the ground is shifting. What must be remembered is that the tremors began not in February 1988, when Daishowa bought the mill, or August 1945, when the Japanese accepted their defeat, but much, much earlier, when those three sailors washed ashore on a rocky beach and were captured, or rescued, by the Northwest's earliest inhabitants, a powerful tribe of whale hunters.

In the past, America called the shots: shipping the Japanese sailors back home with a price on their heads; chasing others out of railroad camps and mines at gunpoint; putting Japanese Americans behind barbed wire when their loyalty was in question. But even these high school students realize that the United States no longer has the power, or the money, to put up fences to keep out the rest of the world. They are learning to speak Japanese because they believe in the power of communication. They are motivated by need.

Port Angeles and Daishowa need each other. The United States and Japan need each other. But need without respect equals resentment. And resentment without understanding is dangerous. Those who treat the U.S.-Japan relationship like a crosstown football rivalry—who trade insults and threats like stadium cheers—should listen to the people of the Olympic Peninsula. They are living with the consequences of false rhetoric and national shortsightedness and see the benefits and the threat of the Pacific Century reflected in the mundane occurrences of their daily lives. In small ways, in the most personal of ways, they are reclaiming their country. Not from the Japanese, who never owned it, but from the weakest part of themselves, the part that saw the world as flat and the ocean as a wall. And in the greatest irony of all, Japan is playing a role in pulling America back from the precipice. In an economy without borders, the futures of the two countries are inextricably linked.

From their very first contacts, the United States and Japan have walked a tightrope between attraction and revulsion, yin and yang, constantly thrown off balance by language barriers, cultural misunderstandings, and egos struggling for control. It is an entanglement of high-pitched emotion worthy of two proud, powerful nations. It has not been, and never will be, easy.

Those entering the uncharted waters of the Pacific Century would be wise to pay heed to those who are forging ahead: Know your destination, study the currents, and never turn your back on the waves.

ACKNOWLEDGMENTS

I N THE END IT IS A collection of words. In the beginning it was an idea. For their help in assisting me from the former to the latter, I owe thanks to many.

First and foremost, I must thank the people of the Olympic Peninsula, particularly the residents of Port Angeles, who gave me the material to breathe life into this book. The following are just some of the many people who made this possible: the employees of Daishowa America, including Steve Taniguchi and Bob Hartley; the staff at Daishowa's Port Angeles mill and their families, including Tad, Fumiko, Akira, and Makoto

Mochizuki, Dave and Marcy Hoglund, Matt Bryant, Ed Adamich, Alyce Hallman, and Parker Holden; Tomiko Brewer; Margaret Crawford; Frank Ducceschi; Eva (Winters) Fowler; David Hagiwara; the late Sam Haguewood; Becky Hall; Jerry Hendricks; Archie and Thelma (Winters) Helgeson; Gaye Knudson; Yosuke and Hiroshi Kobayashi; Rachel Kowalski; Harry and Evelyn Lydiard; the staff at the *Peninsula Daily News*; the students of Port Angeles Senior High School; Lucy Ross; Laura Jo (Winters) Whipple, and John ("Bud") and Doris Willson.

Also helpful in my quest for information were Junko Sakakibara and Noriko Palmer of Japan Entertainment Network of Seattle, Rich Hsu and Ken Nakano of the Japanese American Citizens League, Yoshio Hayashi of Oji Paper Co. Ltd., and Paul Isaki, former director of the Washington State Department of Trade and Economic Development. In Neah Bay, I am indebted to Maria Parker-Pascua and the staff at the Makah Cultural and Research Center, Mary Hunter, and other members of the Makah Nation. And I must make particular note of the many hours Professor Richard McKinnon spent with me sharing his family's past as well as his great love for the two countries he calls home. Also helpful were the research staff at Fort Vancouver, Washington; Betty Tonglau at the Seattle Public Library; and the University of Washington's Suzallo Library.

In Japan, I owe much to the Saito family; the staff of Daishowa Paper Mfg. Co.; the Japan Paper Association; Kyoichi Takado, president of *Pulp and Paper News*; Keizo Kishi, chief editor, *Paper Business Review*; Randy Helton, Youichi Kuroda, and Stephen McKay of Friends of the Earth/Japan and the Japan Tropical Forest Action Network; Patricia Jennings of Baring Securities; and Seiichi Soeda, of the Foreign Press Center in Japan. In Fuji City, my work was made possible by the kind assistance of the staff at Daishowa's Fuji City mill, Satoko Fukushima and George Tokumitsu of BECS, and Anna Saito, who worked as an interpreter.

I can't thank enough Tom and Peggie Osasa, who willingly opened up their past to a stranger.

At the *Seattle Post-Intelligencer*, I am indebted to Publisher J. D. Alexander and National/Foreign Editor Robert Schenet for giving me the time to tackle this project. Katy Khakpour's organizational skills helped keep me on track and smiling, and the library was a valuable resource.

For their unwavering support and child care, I am particularly thankful to my parents, Willy and Eiko Iritani, to Katherine Iritani, Barry Wong, Brian Iritani, and Sally Thompson; the Ainsley clan, in particular Margaret and the late Bert Ainsley, Stuart Ainsley, Jennifer Nunn; Nole Ann Horsey and Mary Stodden. For shepherding these words through their various stages, I am indebted to David Horsey, Sheila Anne Feeney, Sue Hertz, Mary Lynn Lyke, Casey Corr, and Walter Hatch.

For a glorious month of writing and solitude, I thank the Centrum Foundation of Port Townsend, Washington, and for their advice, encouragement, and pasta, I owe much to Keith Raether, Alice Blanchard, and Robert Pyle, an inspirational teacher and author of *Wintergreen* (New York: Charles Scribner's Sons, 1986) and *Thunder Tree: Lessons from a Secondhand Landscape* (Boston: Houghton Mifflin, 1993).

I am grateful to Artist Trust, the Seattle-based art foundation, for providing a grant so I could complete this project.

In Port Angeles, I could not have survived without the generosity and companionship of Lucy Schott and Del Price.

For providing me inspiration at bleak hours of the night, I must thank Melissa Fay Greene for writing *Praying for Sheetrock* (New York: Ballantine Books, 1991), a beautifully crafted work that brought the civil rights movement to life.

Without the perseverance and support of Will Schwalbe, my editor at William Morrow & Company, Inc., this book would not exist today. I could not have asked for a better coach, counselor, and friend. And I would also like to thank Michael Goodman for his careful copyediting.

As live-in editor, chef, and confidant, my husband, Roger Ainsley, kept me sane and well-fed. Without his generosity of mind and spirit, I would not have been able to undertake such an all-consuming project. And to Shaara and Nicholas, my soulmates, I thank you for never failing to remind me of the important things in life: love and laughter.

SUGGESTED
READING

IN ADDITION TO THE BOOKS cited in the Note to the Reader (page 7), here is a listing of other books that pertain to the subjects discussed:

For insight into the early lives of the Makah and the history of the Olympic Peninsula, there is no finer book than *Winter Brothers: A Season at the Edge of America* by Ivan Doig (San Diego and New York: Harvest/Harcourt Brace Jovanovich, 1980). Timothy Egan's book *The Good Rain* (New York: Knopf, 1990) is a well-written foray into the Pacific Northwest psyche.

I have benefited from reading many fine works on the lives of early Asian immigrants to the United States, but I would like to cite a few that were an inspiration. Those were *The Issei: The World of the First Generation Japanese Immigrants, 1885–1924* by Yuji Ichioka (New York: The Free Press, 1988); *Asian America: Chinese and Japanese in the United States Since 1850* by Roger Daniels (Seattle: University of Washington Press, 1988); several articles by Professor Emeritus Frank Miyamoto of the University of Washington; *Joseph Kawamoto: East Meets West in Leland Valley*, Volume 28 of *Witness to the First Century: 1889–1989* by the Jefferson County Historical Society (Port Townsend, Wash.: Jefferson County Historical Society, 1989), and "Undesirables: Early Immigrants and the Anti-Japanese Movement in San Francisco, 1892–1893," by Donald Teruo Hata, Jr. (Ph.D. diss., University of Southern California, 1970).

There are many good books on the relations between the people of the United States and Japan that I have used as resources over the years but among the highlights are *Trading Places* by Clyde Prestowitz, Jr. (New York: Basic Books, 1988); *More Like Us: Putting America's Native Strengths and Traditional Values to Work to Overcome the Asian Challenge* by James Fallows (Boston: Houghton Mifflin, 1989); *The Reckoning* by David Halberstam (New York: William Morrow, 1986); *The Japanese* by Edwin O. Reischauer (Cambridge, Mass.: Belknap/Harvard University Press, 1977); *The Japanese Mind* by Robert C. Christopher (New York: Ballantine Books, 1983); *Japan Before Perry: A Short History* by Conrad Totman (Berkeley: University of California Press, 1981); *Turning Japanese* by David Mura (New York: Atlantic Monthly Press, 1991); *War Without Mercy:*

Race and Power in the Pacific War by John Dower (New York: The New Press, 1993); *In the Realm of a Dying Emperor: A Portrait of Japan at Century's End* by Norma Field (New York: Random House, 1993) and *Talking to High Monks in the Snow* by Lydia Minatoya (New York: HarperCollins, 1992).

INDEX